45

THE *Browsable Classroom*

AN INTRODUCTION TO
E-LEARNING FOR LIBRARIANS

Carolyn B. Noah AND *Linda W. Braun*

Neal-Schuman Publishers, Inc.
NEW YORK   LONDON

Published by Neal-Schuman Publishers, Inc.
100 Varick Street
New York, NY 10013

The paper used in this publication meets the minimum requirements of American National Standard for Information Sciences—Permanence of Paper for Printed Library Materials, ANSI Z39.48-1992.

Printed and bound in the United States of America.

ISBN 1–55570–425–5

Library of Congress Cataloging-in-Publication Data

Noah, Carolyn B.
     The browsable classroom : an introduction to e-learning for librarians / Carolyn B. Noah, Linda W. Braun
          p. cm. — (Neal-Schuman netguide series)
     Includes bibliographical references and index.
     ISBN 1-55570-425-5 (alk. paper)
     1. Libraries and distance education. 2. Distance education.
3. Internet in education. I. Noah, Carolyn. II. Series.

Z718.8 .B73 2002
371.3'58'024092—dc21

                                                        2002044521

Contents

List of Figures

Preface

The Browsable Classroom: An Introduction to E-Learning for Librarians explores a fascinating new world of possibilities for acquiring all types of education—from degree programs to lifelong learning. As innovative uses of the Internet transform learning, they also alter the jobs of the librarians who must meet the ever-changing challenge of serving these new e-learners. Despite its contemporary association with the Internet, distance learning isn't a new concept. Correspondence courses, which have been available for decades, were the first examples of distance learning. They liberated students from the confines of the classroom. For the first time, learners could work on assignments in the comfort of home—on their own schedule, at their own pace. What is new is how the Internet transformed this familiar scenario into a revolutionary new experience.

Picture this: It's late at night and you're sitting at your computer in your pajamas sipping a cup of tea. You log on to the Web site posted for the course you enrolled in by e-mail. Even at this late hour, other students in the class are chatting online. You join a lively discussion about the latest group assignment and how best to complete it. Armed with a good idea of what you need to do next, you browse the Web site and check out your readings—most of it hyperlinked and downloadable. You click on the link to the library and research their electronic capabilities. You even schedule an appointment to meet online with another student and leave an e-mail message for the professor to schedule a talk about the final paper.

This illustration highlights some of the most appealing, flexible features of Web-based distance education. Learners can work on course material on their own schedules and at their own pace. They attend class remotely and meet with other students and instructors online. Learners discuss assignments and other work related to the course in virtual time and space. Web-based distance education gives instructors the chance to communicate with students more than just once a week in a "live" class. For many students and instructors, learning and teaching like this is a dream come true. For others, mastering the technology is a nightmare. Librarians may embrace the e-revolution or shy away from it, but none can afford to ignore it completely.

For many librarians already involved in distance education, *The Browsable Classroom* will show how libraries that support and host distance learning meet the challenge and opportunity of learning to assist users in a whole new dimension. Other librarians, their curiosity piqued about e-learning, will use *The Browsable Classroom* as a map as they venture into uncharted waters. How will the distance learning revolution change my career? Is it something for me to consider for the academic, school, or public library I work in? How might I offer the benefits of distance learning to my users? How do I become knowledgeable about e-learning? How do I prepare for e-learners when they request my services? *The*

Browsable Classroom: An Introduction to E-Learning for Librarians provides answers to these important questions.

In the title, the word *browsable* is a not-quite-made-up word describing the unique distinction of Web-based learning. *Browsing* attempts to describe the way that the digital revolution has changed a fundamental way people take in information and knowledge. In much the same way readers browse a magazine or shoppers browse a store, learners can work through courses in an individual manner. They can travel at their own tempos, revisit sections they want to consider more deeply, and jump ahead when they're ready. Indeed, the Internet and the virtual classroom is a friend to the non-linear learner. *The Browsable Classroom: An Introduction to E-Learning for Librarians* will suggest the best ways to serve the original needs of these distinct users.

Although librarians are the primary audience for *The Browsable Classroom,* educators and students will also learn valuable new skills. Educators will discover how to create successful distance learning experiences and students will learn what it takes to succeed in the distance learning classroom. Each of *The Browsable Classroom*'s seven chapters thoroughly explores a specific facet of distance education that librarians need to understand so they can plan and implement services that benefit distance learners and teachers—and benefit from distance learning opportunities available for librarians.

The first chapter, "Go the Distance: Education Options Online," begins by explaining synchronous and asynchronous learning environments. The strengths and weaknesses of these two primary methods of delivering remote instruction are analyzed. Here you will learn the differences and distinctions by comparing the synchronous methods of real-time chat, compressed video, and face-to-face learning environments to the asynchronous learning environments of discussion boards, templates for surveys and quizzes, note and presentation posting, and video and e-mail.

Chapter 2, "Think Strategically: Successful Distance Education Models for the Library Community," presents a variety of distance learning models to illustrate the scope of e-learning today. You'll look at services for adult learners, like SmartPlanet, that highlight the differences between self-study and teacher-led courses. Two distance learning initiatives—the Exhibits and the Teacher's Lab (developed by the Annenburg/CPB Project)—demonstrate the marriage of text and interactivity and ways to teach students concrete and abstract content via the Web. A great way to understand e-learning is by a close examination of some of the professional courses available to librarians. The American Association of School Librarians (AASL) offers a series of courses covering a variety of topics including searching and navigating the Web and telecollaborative projects. The Young Adult Library Services Association (YALSA) offers an interactive tutorial examining adolescent needs and librarian responses. Innovative courses offered by libraries and librarians include Web-based tutorials that teach searching skills, basic library and reference skills for paraprofessionals, and Web page development. *The Browsable Classroom* surveys some of the best and brightest ideas in e-learning by accredited library and information programs including The University of Chicago, Connecticut State University, and the University of Pittsburgh.

Chapter 3, "Lead On: The Library's Growing Role in Distance Education," will show you how to prepare for the changes inherent in the shift toward e-learning. Whether or not your library or school is preparing to offer distance learning opportunities, every library or school should be ready to support distance learners in need of resources. In addition to offering traditional library services, some libraries agree to be sites for students who lack connectivity to participate from home. Find out how libraries can serve students and teachers who are involved in distance learning and what standards have been set for its delivery. Become acquainted with distance education students and programs. Discover the changing nature of library resources for distance learners: the traditional and non-traditional library roles that support distance learning. Chapter 3 ends with an inquiry into standards for distance learning library services, including copyright and collaboration issues.

Chapter 4, "Be Creative: Effective Education Program Design," will teach you the basics of program design and contrast the challenges of the e-learning environment to traditional models. It takes a great deal of planning, enthusiasm, and energy to create a viable and useful distance learning course. How do you begin? The development of distant learning demands organizational, human, and technical resources and starts by examining the organization in which you operate. You will learn how to balance many considerations: the organization's goal in relationship to the project, the goals for the instructional offering, the availability of expertise, the project's potential audience, and the technological demands. You will learn how to ascertain the skills of the key players—the content expert, the instructional designer, technical expert, and the student tester. You will learn how to determine a potential audience, show how to put the pieces together, and then prepare for the thrill of "going live." Barriers to success and outcomes for first-time distance learning providers conclude the discussion

"Renew and Retool: New Skills for the Distance Educator" is the subject of Chapter 5. Teaching in an electronic environment is very different from teaching in a "live" classroom. *The Browsable Classroom* will show you new ways to select and prepare content. How do you respond to e-mail, facilitate board discussion, and deal with inappropriate communication? Chapter 5 provides useful solutions to the new uncertainties of e-learning and addresses the best way to deal with potentially problematic areas like concerns over student writing style and the most effective ways to help students understand assignments.

Chapter 6, "Handle with Care: Assessment of Distance Education Students' Needs," covers the important issues that students face as they decide whether to enroll in a distance education course and how to proceed once they begin their studies. You will discover the best ways to discover if students have the requisite academic and technological skills to succeed in distance learning before enrollment. Then you will learn what to do once the program begins. Included are checklists for students to stay on track and keep organized, meet online with classmates, handle the demands of technology, and stay motivated.

The last chapter, "Look Ahead: The Future of the Browsable Classroom," summarizes the current world of distance education and points to the potential promise of e-learning. It reviews the expanding options for distance

learners, the need for libraries to collaborate and get involved, and the best ways to build the online learning experience and to teach in the virtual classroom. A glossary
of useful distance education terms completes this guide. A
bibliography is provided which lists books, articles, and
Web sites that are mentioned in the text or are of use to
readers searching for further information about distance
learning.

As technology continues to change, distance learning
opportunities will no doubt evolve as well. The important
questions for librarians, educators, and students are con-
stant. What constitutes a high-quality distance learning
experience? How can educators create these experiences?
What do students need to know when they get involved
in distance learning? *The Browsable Classroom: An Introduction to E-Learning for Librarians* provides the answers
to these questions and more. It establishes the framework
for the successful integration of distance learning into your
future as a teacher or librarian. *The Browsable Classroom*
provides you with the skills that this exciting, new fron-
tier asks of your professional life.

Acknowledgments

We would like to thank the following educators, librarians, and students for taking time to answer our questions as we gathered information for this book: Cheryl McCarthy, Gale Eaton, Jana Bradley, Christine Jenkins, Barbara Kwasnik, Connie Schlotterbeck, Tom Anderson, Kathy Somerville, Susan Farr, Owen Shuman, Susan Lowe, Clare Underwood, Sean Ramsdell, Joan Platt, and Margaret Morrissey.

Chapter 1

Go the Distance:
Education Options Online

What does distance education look like in a library and library education environment?

If you visit the Distance Education Clearinghouse Web site and select the "Definitions" link, one thing quickly becomes apparent—the phrase "distance education" means different things to different people. Nine different definitions are listed on the "Definitions" page of the Web site. A few mention that distance education takes place when a student and teacher are separated by space. Other definitions mention use of technology in the delivery of course content. Some mention that distance education connects students to resources required for learning.

What is consistent in these definitions is the goal to teach students a skill or topic from a distance. This does not mean that students never meet together to talk about course content and skills. As a matter of fact, some of the most successful distance learning programs combine teaching and learning at a distance with face-to-face meetings of students and teachers.

Distance learning does not simply mean that a teacher puts his or her material in an electronic format for students to access. As we discuss in Chapters 3 and 4, effective distance learning requires reformatting or creating content so that it will be useable by students at a distance. Successful distance learning takes into consideration the benefits of technology as an educational tool and balances those benefits with tried and true methods of teaching in a "live" classroom.

Distance learning has been divided into two types of experiences: synchronous learning, in which students and teachers communicate electronically in real time, and asynchronous learning, in which students and teachers communicate electronically but not in real time. Of course, as mentioned above, some distance learning courses combine synchronous and asynchronous delivery so students have the experience of both. Let's look a little more closely at how each of these options plays out in learning and teaching environments specifically for librarians and students in schools of library and/or information technology. In Chapter 2 we talk more generally about different distance learning options for a general adult population and for library students and practicing librarians.

SYNCHRONOUS LEARNING ENVIRONMENTS

Distance education courses that use synchronous delivery methods take advantage of a variety of technologies to provide successful learning experiences for students. These include real-time text and audio chat, use of video technologies such as compressed video (sometimes referred to

Figure 1–1: LEEP: Distance Education Option Home Page.

as PictureTel), and face-to-face meetings of students at the beginning and/or end of courses or the educational program. Examples of each of these follow.

Real-Time Chat

In the online tour of a LEEP class, at The Graduate School of Library and Information Science at the University of Illinois at Urbana-Champaign, Christine Jenkins demonstrates how chat is integrated into a children's literature class. The example displayed on the Web site focuses on a class that discussed the topic of literacy work and young children. Students enrolled in the class logged onto the course Web site before its 6:00 p.m. starting time. When class began, Jenkins read the book *Mike's House* by Julie Sauer. While listening to the text, students were able to "turn the pages" of the book as Jenkins had digitized the images. When the reading was done students broke up into groups and discussed, in real time, the topic for the week. Jenkins writes on the Web site, "An online discussion has a slower pace than a face-to-face discussion, but in 20 minutes each group had laid out a brief thematic program of literacy activities for young children. When we reconvened in virtual 406, each group gave a brief report on their discussion, with other students chiming in with questions and responses" (Jenkins, 1998).

Instructors also use chat as a means of hosting guest speakers in a distance education class. Chat allows students to hear from and talk to experts in a field. Often these are people who students might not have had access to, because of cost or location, in a live class but who are available remotely through the use of real-time chat.

As students in a distance education class may be attending the class from locations around the world, chat events are sometimes scheduled at multiple times during a course week. This allows students in varying time zones to participate at an hour that is appropriate to and convenient for their locality.

Some instructors also use chat as a way of providing office hours to students. Instructors list their weekly hours as they would for classes that take place inside campus facilities. Students can log onto their computers during the time advertised and discuss with their instructor questions and topics related to the content of the class.

Scheduled flexibly, chat offers much of the immediacy of face-to-face conversation and "live" classrooms. Students actively participate in the class chat space to learn from their classmates and the instructor in an instantaneous environment. After a class chat session, students feel they attended a class, covered a topic thoroughly, and received instant feedback from the others involved in the learning experience.

Unfortunately chat has a downside. Students with slow connections to the Internet may miss out on much of the immediacy of the chat experience, as they will need to wait to read or hear what their classmates and instructor are discussing. In classroom chat areas where text is the only mode of communication, students involved are required to think and write quickly so as not to slow down the flow of the class. Those students who are not proficient at this may suffer from not being able to keep up with the conversation. Audio chat of course does not have this same downside. However the technology to use audio chat does require a higher-speed and more stable Internet connection.

As discussed below, one of the benefits of asynchronous learning is that the format provides students with the chance to consider carefully their ideas about the topic prior to discussing it with their classmates. As with traditional classrooms, if students do not have time before the class to read about the topic and think about the issues to be addressed in the chat classroom, they may suffer from an inability to articulate their ideas clearly in the fast-moving chat environment.

PictureTel/Compressed Video

PictureTel (also called compressed video) technology enables students and instructors to communicate in real time using compressed video. In a PictureTel situation, students meet in a location in which the technology is available. The instructor is also in a location with the technology. Class then takes place almost as if it were a standard live classroom. Students can see the instructor on a TV placed somewhere in the classroom and the instructor can see the students on a TV screen. With PictureTel it's not only possible to hear what a student or instructor is saying, but it's also possible to gain insights into the meaning of what's being said through the ability to see the speaker's body language, even though she might be hundreds of miles away.

At the University of Rhode Island Graduate School of Library and Information Studies, instructors use PictureTel to meet with students at remote sites around New England. These remote sites, at institutions of higher learning, house the PictureTel technology and make it available to students. In the University of Rhode Island program, PictureTel has been used to give students at remote locations a chance to do live presentations for their classmates, in other remote locations, and the instructor. For example in the course on library management, students role-play case studies while students at other remote sites, and/or in a classroom on campus, look on. After a presentation all of the students, those viewing the role plays and those presenting the role plays, discuss the issues and concepts presented via PictureTel. When talking about use of PictureTel at the University of Rhode Island Cheryl McCarthy stated, "The live classroom or the compressed video classrooms allow for synchronous communication and dialogue across boundaries and classrooms without the artificiality of reading comments on a bulletin board" (2000).

A compressed video/PictureTel distance learning environment offers the nuances of face-to-face communication but requires that students and teachers assemble in given places and at particular times. For students in the remote location it is sometimes difficult to feel involved in the classroom experience. Although they see the instructor and other classmates in real time, if the monitor being used is too small or the instruction is not interactive enough students can quickly lose interest. The potential for disengagement presents new challenges to the instructor who needs to find methods for keeping students both on and off site involved in the learning experience.

At the same time, technology similar to PictureTel allows distance learning students to take part in an educational experience from a site that is fairly close to their home. They also get to interact with a group of students in the same general location, which makes it possible to have face-to-face meetings outside of class time to work on projects together.

As with chat, using technology like PictureTel in distance learning requires the instructor to think carefully about the benefits of the technology and how to harness these benefits to provide useful and appropriate learning experiences. Using PictureTel for student presentations is an effective means of using the technology. However, if compressed video is simply used to bring talking head lectures to students its impact and use will be much less advantageous to learning.

Face-to-Face Learning Environments

LEEP and the University of Rhode Island both require face-to-face meetings with students at various times during their course work. Students enrolled in the University of Rhode Island are required to fulfill a 15-hour residency requirement. Similarly, instructors visit students enrolled in the Regional Program at the off-campus sites that act as hosts to the students.

The LEEP program Web site states, "Students begin LEEP with a 12-day campus stay. Each following semester of enrollment, students travel to UIUC for a three- to five-day stay on campus" (Jenkins, 1998).

At LEEP the initial stay on campus acts as an orientation to the program and the technology that students will use. In most instances where face-to-face meetings are required, the institution has determined that these meetings help both faculty and students become familiar and comfortable with each other and the program they are embarking on, or in which they are already involved. Cheryl McCarthy, at the University of Rhode Island, states that "at least one face-to-face class allows for the opportunity to personally connect names and faces and share experiences in a social-cultural classroom environment" (McCarthy, 2000).

When the Central Massachusetts Regional Library System (CMRLS) offered a basic library techniques distance education course on library administration they used a sandwich approach to course delivery. Students enrolled in the course were required to attend two face-to-face meetings, one at the beginning of the course and one at the end of the course. In the middle those enrolled took part in asynchronous online learning activities via the course Web site. The evaluation of the CMRLS course found that one of the successes was the sandwich approach to learning. The evaluation states, "Students appreciated having an opportunity to meet as a group. Not only did they think it was important to meet their classmates face-to-face, they also thought it was necessary to meet the instructor in order to ask questions in a 'live' classroom environment" (Braun, 2000:3).

A face-to-face component for distance learning is an excellent way to bring a group of students together to make sure they have the information and resources required in order to get the most from the distance learning experience. If an institution does not require a face-to-face element in its program, it should develop other methods for making sure that students are prepared for taking courses remotely and for handling problems that might arise during a course period. Without this preparation, students may find they are floundering with no idea about what is expected of them or how they should proceed. You can read more about methods for ensuring student success in Chapters 5 and 6.

ASYNCHRONOUS LEARNING ENVIRONMENTS

Many institutions that provide distance education opportunities for students use courseware as the interface for both synchronous and asynchronous teaching and learning. This courseware acts as a portal to the distance learning courses for both faculty and students (see the sidebar on the next page to learn more about courseware). Blackboard and WebCT are two popular vendors of this

More About Courseware

Throughout this book you'll find that we mention courseware. Many educational institutions use this software interface as a gateway to online learning. When a student logs onto the institution's distance learning Web site he or she accesses his or her own personal main page that includes links to the courses he or she is taking as well as other useful resources provided by the sponsoring institution.

Courseware allows an institution to make sure that all of the distance learning courses they offer have the same look, feel, and interactive components. Standard in a courseware package are discussion boards, chat rooms, areas for posting links to external Web sites, and administrative features for the course instructor.

When using courseware, students and instructors can attach documents—including pictures and word processing—from their own computers to the discussion board.

Another common feature of courseware packages is an area that students can use to hand in assignments. Sometimes called a "digital dropbox," this is the place where a student submits an assignment to the instructor. The instructor can pick up the assignment from the digital dropbox, grade it, and then send it back to the student's own dropbox. This feature makes the submitting, grading, and returning of assignments a simple process.

The administrative tools included in a courseware package usually allow an instructor to keep track of student grades and participation. Many courseware packages provide statistics on how many times a particular student has accessed the various features of the site. This is useful for instructors in keeping track of class participation. The feature also comes in handy for students also if they want to keep track of how often they post messages on the discussion board. Students can then make sure they are keeping up with the course as they should be.

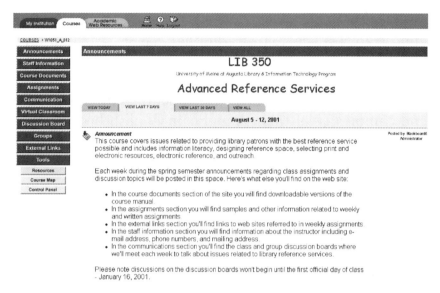

Figure 1–2: LIB 350: Advanced Reference Services Home Page (University of Maine at Augusta).

courseware. Each provides an interface for real-time chat and for asynchronous learning with features such as discussion boards, templates for quizzes and surveys, and areas to post notes and presentations. (See Figure 1–2.) Some institutions also use video and CD-ROM technologies and electronic mailing lists. The sections below highlight how each of these methods is used in asynchronous learning environments.

Discussion Boards

When discussing online instruction at Syracuse University's School of Information Studies, Jana Bradley, the director of the library science program and an instructor in the program, made this statement, "The international students in my face-to-face classes who are not facile in English are almost always silent. In traditional classes, I would only glimpse the depth of their understanding and their mental processes through the end-of-term papers. With online discussion, often these students are able to express the depth and complexity of their thoughts in English because they have the time to work it all out carefully. As a result, they are full intellectual participants in the class and become, as a result, much more an integrated part of the group" (Bradley, 2000).

Many instructors who teach distance education courses have learned the power of using discussion boards to create high-quality learning environments. In an asynchronous learning the discussion board is often the central point for student learning. Students and instructors go to boards to brainstorm ideas related to course content, ask questions about topics discussed, and find out what others think about ideas associated with the course content.

Discussion boards have the advantage of eliciting response at the learners' convenience. As Jana Bradley pointed out, they also provide students with an opportunity to take time to consider carefully the topic up for discussion. They also pose the challenge for learners and instructors of piled-up responses to read and answer within a defined timeline.

You can read more about the facilitation and integration of discussion boards in Chapter 5.

Templates for Surveys and Quizzes

There are instances when course content requires that students fill out a quiz or survey. In an asynchronous environment the instructor creates the quiz or survey, makes it available on the course Web site, and then students take the quiz or survey within an allotted period of time. This format is used for an information literacy course taught in the University of Maine at Augusta's Library and Information Technology program. The four-week, one-credit course, required for all library and information technology students, uses quizzes and surveys to teach information literacy skills—from developing a search strategy to citing electronic resources. When students submit their answers, the instructor has immediate access to them via the course online grade book. He or she then looks over the submissions and e-mails students with follow-up information or points out areas a student needs to focus on in order to gain a better understanding of the course content.

In a distance learning environment, where the instructor cannot answer questions immediately about quiz content, it is extremely important to make sure that questions asked on quizzes and surveys are clear and unambiguous. As with pen-and-paper quizzes, this format for assessing student learning may be off-putting to some types of learners. For both reasons, instructors need to be careful about the use of quizzes and surveys in remote learning environments. They should not be the only method for assessing learning and should be balanced with opportunities for synchronous or asynchronous class participation. In all instances where quizzes and surveys are used, students need the chance to ask questions and receive feedback on quiz and survey content.

Note and Presentation Posting

Many instructors in distance education programs use the course Web site to post the course syllabus, class notes, and sometimes PowerPoint or similar presentations. Over the past couple of years Gale Eaton, an instructor at the University of Rhode Island Graduate School of Library and Information Studies has posted her class notes as Power-Point presentations on the course Web site. She found out from students that " . . . they prefer text to PowerPoint for my notes, so I take the outlines that I used to embroider in class and I write out the embroidery. It takes a while but it's enjoyable" (Eaton, 2000).

By posting class notes, the course syllabus, and presentations instructors provide students with the same kinds of tools and resources they use when taking a "live" course. Students can use these materials to learn about the content and keep up with what's required. In Chapter 6 you can read more about how to keep students on task through the use of the class Web site.

Video and E-Mail

The Web isn't the only tool used in asynchronous learning environments. For example, at the University of Maine at Augusta, some faculty in the Library and Information Technology program develop videos that include course lectures, introductory information about the instructor and the course, and interviews with librarians in the field. These are mailed to students enrolled as a part of their course materials at the beginning of the semester. Students are assigned to watch different portions of the videotapes as a part of their weekly readings and assignments.

As discussed above in the section on PictureTel, it's important for instructors who use video to think carefully about the most effective type of content to deliver in this fashion. As video is a visual medium it should only be used to deliver content that deserves and requires a visual presentation. One example might be a tour of a library in order to demonstrate a particular type of layout or architecture. Others might be a series of skits that present customer service dos and don'ts or an interview with someone who is unavailable to students via chat or on the class discussion board.

When PictureTel is used in distance learning, students usually meet on a regular basis to enhance their learning experiences. This social aspect is lost when students use videos delivered directly to their homes. In most instances students watch them in complete isolation—without the benefits of classmates being in the same room during the viewing. Consequently it is vitally important that the use of video be carefully considered and used primarily to provide students with a learning experience in which they would not otherwise be able to take part. If students are required to watch videotaped talking head lectures from week to week it is very likely they will quickly lose interest in the course content and the success of their learning will be jeopardized.

Some instructors use electronic mailing lists as a means of communicating with students in distance education courses. In these situations a mailing list is created for a particular course. Anyone who is enrolled in the course or is course faculty can send a message to the entire list. In some situations faculty use electronic mailing lists in place of online discussion boards as a means of communicating with and between students. Discussion lists similarly offer the same value and challenge as using discussion boards.

CONCLUSION

When defining distance education it's important to consider that different models exist and that some courses use synchronous methods, some use asynchronous methods, and others use a combination of the two. There are even instances in which "live" classes make use of a course Web site in order to create a one-stop location for students to access course materials and resources.

High-quality distance education takes into account that certain types of content require a synchronous format in which students can consider a topic with fellow students and the instructor in real time. In other instances providing students with longer periods of time to consider a topic and then respond electronically to classmates and the instructor is advantageous.

Providing distance education students with face-to-face orientation sessions is advantageous in helping students acclimate to the world of online learning. Similarly, creating a course Web site gives students and instructors a place to go to keep track of course requirements, read course notes and presentations, and take part in synchronous or asynchronous discussions. The course Web site becomes the classroom for students enrolled in a distance education course. In the best of all possible worlds, instructors and learners benefit from experiences that blend both asynchronous with synchronous instruction. In these situations, students profit from material presented in a variety of formats and from content delivered in the way that is most appropriate for student understanding of the topic.

By now you may be wondering how one decides the best method for delivering course content. Read on. You'll learn more about developing and delivering content in Chapters 4 and 5.

REFERENCES

Bradley, Jana. 2000. Telephone interview with Linda Braun, Syracuse, N.Y., December 18.

Braun, Linda W. 2000. *Massachusetts Online Distance Education for Library Staff: MODELS Evaluation of Online Electronic Components*, June.

Eaton, Gale, 2000. Telephone interview with Linda Braun, Kingston, R.I., October 21.

Jenkins, Christine. 1998. *The LEEP Experience: An Instructor's Perspective* [Online]. Available: http://leep.lis.uiuc.edu/demos/jenkins/text/textonly.html [13 December 2000].

McCarthy, Cheryl. 2000. Telephone interview with Linda Braun, Kingston, R.I., November 27.

Chapter 2

Think Strategically: Successful Distance Education Models for the Library Community

The American Library Association (ALA) Web site lists 37 programs at accredited library and information science institutions in the United States that provide distance learning opportunities. This listing includes programs with satellite campuses that require a student's physical presence, on a regular basis, and programs offered entirely at a distance. In this chapter, we'll look at the types of courses available online including courses and tutorials available for adult learners, through the American Library Association, those sponsored and/or created by libraries and librarians, and those at accredited programs in library and information science. The chapter concludes with thoughts about what the future might bring to the world of distance learning and library education.

COURSES FOR ADULTS LEARNERS

On the Web you will find a wide array of courses and tutorials. There are courses on everything from creating Web pages to using e-mail and from life in the Middle Ages to principles of geometry. In this section we look at a few of these offerings.

SmartPlanet

SmartPlanet.com specializes in courses on everything from successful Internet searching to biodiversity. You have two options for accessing course content: Paying a $15.95 per month membership fee provides unlimited access to courses that cost less than $19.95. A "free" membership gives you the ability to pay for courses on a per-course basis.

After registering at SmartPlanet you have two different learning options: self-study or instructor led. We'll look at the self-study option first.

Self-study and instructor-led courses at SmartPlanet

Once you register for a self-study course you gain access to the course Web site. On the site you will find a list of lessons, with links, for the course. These lessons make up the course content. Sometimes lessons include interactive features that allow you to take notes and print out information gathered as a part of one or more of the lessons. In the self-study courses at SmartPlanet, students do not have any interaction with an instructor or fellow students. As a matter of fact, it's likely two students are not taking the course at the same time.

On the other hand, instructor-led courses encourage course participation and communication among students and instructors. (At SmartPlanet, instructor-led courses are only available in the area of computers and the Internet.) All assignments in these courses are posted on the course discussion board. Students view the board to learn what is required and also post messages for the instructor and classmates. This framework is similar to discussion boards used in asynchronous classrooms as discussed in Chapter 1.

A feature of the SmartPlanet discussion boards that students find helpful are the icons associated with different messages. For example, an apple icon denotes that the instructor for the course posted the item, a computer mouse icon denotes that the discussion board moderator posted the message, and an icon of a star denotes that it's an important message from the instructor that everyone should read. This visual system aids students in filtering through the discussion board and making good decisions about which messages to read and when to read them. This is particularly useful when there are a large number of postings to consider.

Annenberg/CPB Project

Two of the distance learning initiatives sponsored by the Annenberg/CPB Project are the Exhibits and Teacher's Lab. These offerings are entirely self-paced and use interactive features in order to aid learning. These interactive features take the place of the discussion boards used by SmartPlanet and many educational institutions. We'll look at the two different learning Web sites provided by the Annenberg/CPB Project separately.

ANNENBERG/CPB PROJECT EXHIBITS

Each of the Exhibits combines text with interactive learning components in order to help visitors deepen their understanding of a particular topic. Exhibit topics include the Middle Ages, physics, statistics, filmmaking, and the Renaissance. The jumping off point for each of the exhibits are videos in the Annenberg/CPB collection.

If you look closely at the Exhibit about statistics, "Polls: What Do the Numbers Tell Us," you can see how text and interactivity are joined to encourage learning. When you access the first screen of the Exhibit, you are asked to complete a survey about your personal experiences with polls and polling. This survey is designed to start you thinking about the topics covered in the Exhibit. After completing the survey, the results of which are displayed at the end of the Exhibit, you enter the Exhibit proper where you learn about a fictitious political campaign. As you learn about the campaign you are asked to consider a variety of issues related to polling and politics.

It is the marriage between text and interactivity that makes this Exhibit work. The fictitious campaign is presented simultaneously with information about the science of polling. When a new idea is discussed (margin of error or random sampling, for example), you have the opportunity to explore the idea interactively in order to see how it actually works. For example, when reading about random sampling you get to create your own random sample by selecting voter attributes including political affiliation, age, gender, and income. The opportunity to actually try out the science and techniques discussed in the Exhibit allows you to actively participate in learning and as a result gain a better understanding of the content.

TEACHER'S LAB

While the Annenberg/CPB Project Exhibits are specifically geared toward the general adult population, the Teacher's Lab is designed for teachers. Specifically, they were produced for math and science teachers as an opportunity to gather new ideas about teaching mathematic and scientific concepts. Each of the four Teacher's Labs covers a different topic including light, patterns, and geometry. These Labs use the same type of interactive features as the Exhibits to provide teachers with an opportunity to try out new teaching techniques.

Let's look at the Teacher's Lab called "Shape and Space in Geometry" to see how another type of text and interactivity work together. As the title suggests, this Lab is divided into two distinct sections: shape and space. When entering each section you are provided with an overview of the content addressed. You then can pick one of three "activities" on the topic. If you select "Shapes," you will be able to investigate the symmetry of quilts, mapping and coordinates, and the properties of proportion

In the "Quilts" activity you first read about why and how quilts present opportunities for teaching students about symmetry. You then read about the types of symmetry covered in the activity. After this brief overview you get to try your hand at matching a quilt's symmetry.

A quilt block is presented on the page. You must determine what type of symmetry to use before you match that symmetry. You are then provided with a series of quilt pieces that you use to fill in an empty block. If you place a quilt piece in the wrong place on the block it remains in place. However, you will begin to notice as more pieces are added that the symmetry you are creating does not match that of the original block provided.

Teachers who try the Quilt activity get the chance to consider the thinking skills required in teaching students about symmetry. The technology allows the teacher to try his or her ideas out, see what works and doesn't work, and revise his or her thoughts about the best way to teach a concept or idea.

Many of the Teacher's Lab activities invite the visitor to post their ideas about what they learned in the activity and about teaching a particular concept or idea. These entries by teachers demonstrate another powerful opportunity that distance learning provides: Learners from around the globe can discuss ideas in order to learn what others have to say about a topic and as a result enhance and extend their learning.

COURSES OFFERED FROM THE AMERICAN ASSOCIATION OF SCHOOL LIBRARIANS AND THE YOUNG ADULT LIBRARY SERVICES ASSOCIATION

Throughout the school year, the American Association of School Librarians (AASL) offers a series of courses for librarians as a part of their ICONnect project. These courses cover a variety of topics including navigating the Web, searching, and telecollaborative projects. Each course takes place over a four-week period and students select one of two ways for participating. By registering for a course a student receives a lesson via e-mail for each of the weeks in which the course takes place. If a student prefers not to register, he or she can visit the course Web site to read the lessons and check out the resources listed. An archive

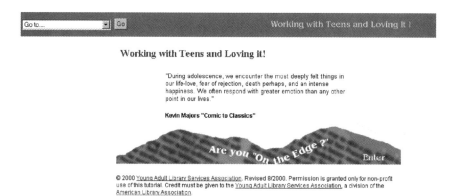

Figure 2–1: YALSA Online Tutorial: Working with Teens and Loving It.

of each of the courses is maintained so even if a student does not take part in the course, when it is first offered, he or she can still take advantage of the material.

As a means of educating librarians about the library service needs of teens, the Young Adult Library Services Association (YALSA) developed an online tutorial for its members. The interactive tutorial, which is only available to YALSA members, combines information about the developmental needs of adolescents with interactive components that help librarians understand the information provided (see Figure 2–1). For example, after the tutorial explains the developmental needs of adolescents, visitors to the site are asked a series of questions about why teens like to participate in certain types of events and why they display particular behaviors. The tutorial ends with ideas on how libraries can meet teen developmental needs through their programs and services.

Each of these online offerings uses technology differently in their delivery of online learning opportunities. ICONnect lessons connect librarians with information to help them integrate technology successfully into the school setting. These text-based lessons do not provide users with opportunities to interact with the content; however, they do present original content so librarians can learn the material in their own time and at their own pace. In many instances it is content that might not otherwise be available to a librarian.

YALSA's Web-based tutorial allows YALSA members to not only read about the topic but also interact with the content in order to advance their learning of the subject matter. As with ICONnect, librarians can use this tutorial to learn the content at their own pace and in their own time. The interactive components give learners an extra opportunity for considering the content and making sure they understand the information presented.

COURSES OFFERED BY LIBRARIES AND LIBRARIANS

Many library institutions develop course offerings for library staff and/or the customers they serve. The most common of these are tutorials on using computers and the Internet successfully. The University at Albany Libraries Web site lists a series of Internet tutorials on "Using and Searching the Web" that includes topics like how to connect to the Internet and Boolean searching. The Ithaca College Library created a Web site titled ICYouSee, which covers topics including "What Can You Do On the World Wide Web" and "What Went Wrong or Why Did It Do That?"

"Bare Bones 101: A Basic Tutorial on Searching the

Web" was created by Ellen Chamberlain, head librarian and full professor at the University of South Carolina, Beaufort. This tutorial is made up of 20 lessons covering definitions of search engines and directories, Boolean searching, search troubleshooting, and details about specific search tools (from Yahoo! to Google). Each lesson explains a particular skill or concept and ends with an assignment for gaining a fuller understanding of the topic covered. For example, the lesson on "Creating a Search Strategy" includes this assignment: "Select a search engine, and try searching the following keywords in this order: 1.Woodstock, 2.Woodstock 1969 3.Woodstock 1969 Grateful Dead" (University of South Carolina Beaufort Library, 2001).

Bare Bones 101 is a good model of breaking down a topic into concrete segments (mind-sized bites) and developing tips and tricks for successfully completing a task. The assignments are a useful means of providing students with direction to help them make sure they understand the information presented in the tutorial.

As with the ICONnect tutorials mentioned above, the University of Albany tutorials, ICYouSee, and Bare Bones 101 courses provide users with the ability to learn a topic at their own pace and on a convenient schedule. Unlike the ICONnect tutorial, however, these sites do not allow visitors to interact with the content or receive feedback regarding the topics covered and their own learning.

The Central Kansas Library System created a series of Web-based training tutorials on everything from mouse skills to e-mail to Internet searching. Many of these tutorials are interactive and give users a chance to try their hand at the concepts discussed. For example, the tutorial on mouse skills, "Mousercise," gives the visitor step-by-step instructions on using the mouse and the only way to move forward in the tutorial is to successfully follow the instructions. Similarly, the tutorial on how Web searching works gives students a chance to see the growth of a subject tree through the simple click of their mouse. The technology used is simple, but the combination of text and content manipulation helps provide students with successful learning opportunities.

Before discussing three other tutorials created by librarians, let's first look at some of the "Tips for Developing Effective Web-Based Instruction" developed by the Association of College & Research Libraries (ACRL). Included on the list of tips are the following:

- Outline the objectives and outcomes clearly to establish purpose and realistic expectations.
- Provide a clearly defined structure that:
  a) reflects the objectives of the tutorial and
  b) allows for both linear and nonlinear learning, so students can review sections and/or select the pathways that best meet their needs.
- Include interactive exercises (active learning) such as with simulations, manipulation of objects, interactive quizzes, or the direct application of principles. These will encourage problem solving by students and allow them to:
  a) practice/respond to what is taught
  b) self-assess their learning
  c) engage in "deep learning" (understanding the meaning) rather than "surface learning" (memorization and regurgitation)
  d) receive feedback.

- Give attention to the concepts behind the mechanics so that information skills are applicable to other search interfaces.
- Incorporate contemporary language and topics, be as succinct as possible, and don't be afraid to entertain (Association of College & Research Libraries, 2000).

Below we discuss three online tutorials created by librarians that demonstrate effective use of technology for teaching a specific set of skills in a distance learning environment. For each we also mention how it successfully integrates one or more of the tips outlined by ACRL above.

Online Tutorials from the Three Rivers Regional Library System

The Three Rivers Regional Library System developed a series of online tutorials for staff at libraries served by the system. There are tutorials in basic library and reference skills for paraprofessional employees and a course on Web page development. The Three Rivers Regional Library System provides certificates of completion for library staff members that finish a tutorial.

Each of these tutorials provides students with information on a particular topic and includes exercises for learning more about the content. For example, in the LIB 101 tutorial (which covers library basics) the section on "What is a Library?" focuses on the library's mission statement and students are asked to locate the mission statement for the library in which they work. In the 101 Reference tutorial, as students learn about the different types of questions people ask, they are required to complete the following exercise: "Locate your library's Reference and Ready Reference collections. If there are separate areas, tables, or computer areas, make a map. Scan the titles of the books in ready reference. What's the most unusual item there? Are there other materials such as maps, pamphlets, phone books, pamphlet files, microforms, or computer databases?" (Three Rivers Regional Library System, 1999).

Each of the Three Rivers tutorials also includes a section for supervisors that provides an overview of the purpose of the lessons, technical notes, and information on the responsibility of the supervisor. As these tutorials do not include interactive components that allow students to submit information and receive feedback electronically, it is important that someone at the library, most likely the staff person's supervisor, is aware of the content of the course and is ready to look over the work the librarian completes for the course. In this way the Three Rivers tutorials combine online distance learning with face-to-face instruction. The librarian/student has the benefit of the content provided by the library system, while at the same time is able to communicate with colleagues at their own library to gain more insight into the content and feedback on the work they complete.

FALCON: An Interactive Web Tutorial

Each page of the FALCON tutorial, created by Bowling Green State University, asks students to consider an aspect of using the library catalog and to interact with the content by answering questions about locating library resources. Tutorial pages also integrate the library catalog interface into the design so students aren't learning about

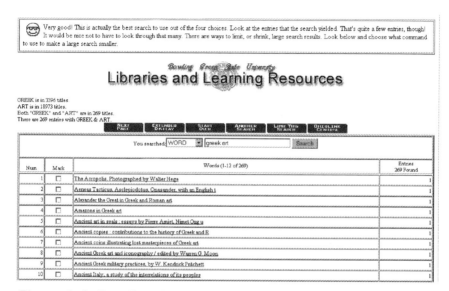

Figure 2–2: Bowling Green State University Libraries and Learning Resources: Learning about Subject/Keyword Searching with FALCON.

the catalog out of context or without actually seeing how it works.

For example in the tutorial section on subject headings and keywords, students are asked to determine what phrase to use in order to find information on Greek art. You can see the resulting page in Figure 2–2. The top of the page provides feedback to the student on their answer while the bottom of the page displays a section of the library catalog.

Throughout the Bowling Green tutorial students receive feedback on their correct and incorrect answers. When an answer is incorrect they are invited to try again. In this way FALCON meets the criteria set out by ACRL related to interactive exercises that provide practice and feedback. What the Bowling Green tutorial does lack is a structure that allows for linear and non-linear learning. Students cannot select a particular section of the tutorial to learn about a specific area of content. Instead they must go through the lessons in a linear fashion, completing each section or topic area before moving onto the next.

TILT: Texas Information Literacy Tutorial

TILT is a tutorial created for students at the University of Texas that provides several good examples of what to include in a distance learning experience. Under the "Project Summary" section of the Web site the authors write:

> Unlike many library tutorials on the Web, this interactive tutorial provides a "problem based learning" environment. A problem-based approach has, we believe, implications for how the computer can be used as a teaching tool. Rather than drilling students about library jargon through a linear presentation, students will be presented with basic concepts and encouraged to work through a series of interactions. We feel that one of the greatest assets of the Web as an educational tool is its interactivity, where user input affects outcomes and results in multiple ways. We plan on giving significant attention to the instructional design and graphical layout, as a means to counter the dry formalism much of the content may otherwise succumb to in a more traditional presentation (University of Texas Digital Libraries, 2000).

On the first TILT page, students can select either TILT Lite (which requires no plug-ins) or Full TILT (which requires plug-ins such as Shockwave). This choice of connection demonstrates that the creators of TILT were thinking about their audience. They realized that not all users would have high-speed access nor would all computers accessing the site be able to use certain plug-ins. In this way, TILT also ensures that students do not have to worry about their technology capabilities and access at the same time they are learning new content.

One of the highlights of TILT, however, is that all of the pieces work together—content and design—so that students are presented with an attractive, even entertaining, learning experience. TILT certainly succeeds at meeting the ACRL criteria that reads, "Incorporate contemporary language and topics, be as succinct as possible, and don't be afraid to entertain" (ACRL, 2000).

The site is organized into a series of modules that include selecting, searching, and evaluating resources. In each module, students have opportunities for interacting with the content. For example, in the evaluation module students learn about how materials are organized in the library. They are told how the Library of Congress classification system works and then have to determine where a book with a particular Library of Congress classification should be shelved. When the student makes a selection he or she is given feedback about why the shelving selection is correct or incorrect. The feedback provided embeds information about the Library of Congress classification system and how it works, giving students another opportunity for learning something about the organizational structure of the library.

On almost every page of TILT students interact with the content by answering questions, simply pointing their

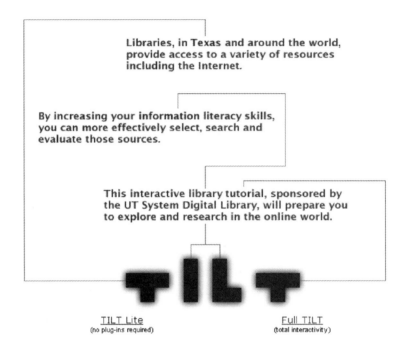

Libraries, in Texas and around the world, provide access to a variety of resources including the Internet.

By increasing your information literacy skills, you can more effectively select, search and evaluate those sources.

This interactive library tutorial, sponsored by the UT System Digital Library, will prepare you to explore and research in the online world.

TILT Lite
(no plug-ins required)

Full TILT
(total interactivity)

Resources for Librarians and Educators

Copyright 1998-2001. The University of Texas System Digital Library. This material may be reproduced, distributed, or incorporated only subject to the terms and conditions set forth in the TILT Open Publication License. (The latest version is available at http://tilt.lib.utsystem.edu/yourtilt/agreement.html.)

Figure 2–3: Texas Information Literacy Tutorial (TILT) Home Page.

mouse in order to see something on the screen change, or listening to sound effects and the reading of text. TILT engages the students in their learning and as a result it is more likely that the information presented will be remembered. At the end of each module students take a quiz on the topic they just studied. Immediate feedback is provided once they submit their quiz answers and students enrolled in the University are able to e-mail their results to instructors in order to "prove" they have completed one or more modules.

TILT is one of the online library tutorials that most completely fulfills the criteria set out by ACRL. Not only does the site use contemporary language and entertain, as mentioned above, but each module provides a clearly defined structure and set of goals along with giving students lots of opportunity for interacting with the content and gaining feedback on their learning (see Figure 2–3).

Tutorials as discussed in this section are a small component of the distance learning opportunities available to librarians and students. Let's take a look at the larger world of distance learning by looking at what is available at schools of library and information science.

COURSES OFFERED BY ACCREDITED LIBRARY AND INFORMATION PROGRAMS

In Chapters 3 through 6 we discuss several different distance learning programs available from accredited library and information science programs in the United States. In this chapter we provide a basic overview of what some of these institutions currently offer.

If you look at the ALA listing of distance learning library and information science programs, you'll find that each program includes a notation related to course delivery method. These include:

- A list of locations where courses are offered at satellite campuses.
- The headings Online MLS, Location Independent, and

Internet all referring to some aspect of distance learning that is Web-based. (Some of these require time spent on campus and some do not.)

For the purposes of this chapter we will focus on a few programs that deliver distance learning primarily via the Web with or without an on-campus requirement. Many programs offer courses in a distance learning environment but do not allow students to complete all of their degree requirements remotely. As discussed in later chapters, institutions like Syracuse University and The University of Illinois Urbana-Champaign require students to visit the campus for orientation sessions and/or for a specific period of time during each semester. Similarly, many institutions offer Web-based components as an enhancement to their face-to-face classes. This means that during the class week students not only attend a "live" class but they also log onto the course Web site on a regular basis to participate in online discussions and other activities.

In the fall of 1999, Connecticut State University announced that it would offer a master's degree in library science in a distance learning format.

Connecticut State University

The Master of Library Science is the first degree program offered online by Connecticut State University. The program, which requires students complete a minimum of 36 credit hours, is available completely in a Web-based learning format. The University uses eCollege courseware as the interface that students use in order to access and post assignments and communicate with classmates and their instructors.

The Department of Information and Library Science provides an Online Learning Support section as a part of their departmental Web site. Included in this section are useful materials for students contemplating, or enrolled in, distance learning courses. These include online course syllabi (several of which include information on assignments, readings, and course expectations), participation guidelines for online students (which include information on class participation, online conduct, course access, and personal involvement and time), and resources used in the courses offered in the distance learning format.

This material provides students with the information they need in order to make good decisions about their own online learning. With this information in hand, students can decide if a course is right for their needs, if they are going to be able to participate as required in a course, and what the institution's expectations are for students taking courses at a distance. By providing this information to students the university is helping to ensure there will be a limited number of surprises as students go through the MLS program. (See Chapter 6 for more information about the distance learning student.)

University of Pittsburgh

In the winter of 2001 the University of Pittsburgh announced the FastTrack MLIS program. The program Web site states, "FT/MLIS students will begin the program as part of a cohort of peers that will move through the program together. Each new cohort will begin with an orientation in the summer term that introduces students to the program, faculty, and to one another, provides 'hands-on'

computer training, and builds camaraderie and a cooperative learning network among students and faculty. The students in the cohort will also spend time together with their
instructors in learning experiences over a weekend each
term after the initial summer term orientation" (University of Pittsburgh School of Information Sciences, 2001).

This model of an orientation session and follow-up
weekend onsite instruction is one that is used by other distance learning programs and has proved to be successful.
The orientation ensures that students have the requisite
technology skills in order to complete the program and also
allows all those involved to get to know each other outside of the distance learning environment.

WHAT'S NEXT

Schools that offer distance learning programs in library and
information science are beginning to consider methods of
cooperation and collaboration. Staff at these schools are
thinking about ways in which a student enrolled in one
distance learning program can take a course from another
distance learning program and receive appropriate credit
toward his or her degree. When this becomes a reality, students will have a wide array of opportunities for earning
a degree that meets their particular needs and interests. For
example, imagine that a student named Stan decides that
a particular library and information science program will
provide him with the skills he needs in order to pursue his
career. However, Stan decides that he would like to learn
more about youth services librarianship and knows that
his institution of choice doesn't offer many courses in that

area. What Stan can do is take a course from another accredited distance learning program in library and information science and have the credits received from that course
transferred to his "home" institution.

When cooperative agreements between programs allow
for this kind of movement between institutions, we will
most likely see programs that develop a strong identity
along a particular area of librarianship and/or information
technology. Some institutions might specialize in youth services, others might specialize in information literacy, and
others might focus on academic librarianship. Students will
be able to enroll in an institution with a focus that meets
their particular needs. They'll also have the opportunity
to enroll in courses at other institutions where there are
strengths in areas of librarianship that complement their
home institution's catalog and help to fill their individual
learning goals.

CONCLUSION

Looking over the distance learning offerings of libraries,
library systems, and schools of library and information science, one must conclude that we are still in an early stage
of their development and delivery. The range in available
content in a distance learning format is wide. At the low
end of the scale are simple point and click interfaces in
which students read content on the screen to learn about
a topic. At the high end of the scale are high-tech interactive tutorials in which students constantly and consistently
interact with the information presented.

Schools of library and information science are testing the

waters to see what the best methods are for delivering distance learning to students enrolled in their programs. Program offerings and delivery methods vary from Web-enhanced courses to complete master's of library and information science programs online. In between are programs that offer distance learning with an on-campus component.

Undoubtedly, in the near future more and more institutions will explore how they can meet their customers' needs through distance learning. By looking at those who have gone before they will learn what they need to know in order to create high-quality distance learning experiences.

REFERENCES

Association of College & Research Libraries Instruction Section Methods Committee. 2000. *Tips for Developing Effective Web-Based Library Instruction* [Online]. Available www.lib.vt.edu/istm/Web TutorialsTips.html [22 January 2001].

Three Rivers Regional Library System. 2000. *Workshops and Training* [Online]. Available: www.colosys.net/three/training.htm [22 January 2001].

University of Pittsburgh School of Information Sciences. 2001. *FastTrack MLIS* [Online]. Available: http://mctell.sis.pitt.edu/fasttrack/ [22 January 2001].

University of South Carolina Beaufort Library. 2001. "Bare Bones 101 Lesson 6: Creating a Search Strategy" [Online]. Available: www.sc.edu/beaufort/library/lesson6.html [11 August 2001].

The University of Texas System Digital Libraries. 2000. *TILT* [Online]. Available: http://tilt.lib.utsystem.edu/ [22 January 2001].

Chapter 3

Lead On: The Library's Growing Role in Distance Education

School and public librarians, some with little preparation, have recently found their libraries acting as the learning resource centers for high school and college distance learners. States from Florida (The Florida High School) to Massachusetts (The Virtual High School) have established online courses to give secondary students access to an array of courses unavailable locally. Students at postsecondary institutions span the continent and more, so there's no predicting in what locality, or when a learner will present himself at a local library looking for information.

Where there are learners it's likely there are teachers. Identifying and supplying the resources distance education instructors need to do their jobs puts a new spin on traditional services. Among these are helping teachers to orient their students and selecting and accessing resources. In particular, interlibrary loan can take on a whole new dimension.

Though distance learning is a relatively new phenomenon in public and school library settings, electronic communication has enhanced distance learning in institutions of higher education for over a decade. In 1997–98, there were an estimated 1,661,100 enrollments in all distance education courses, and 1,363,670 enrollments in college-level, credit-granting distance education courses, with most at the undergraduate level (U.S. Department of Education, National Center for Educational Statistics, 1999). As a result, academic librarians are much more seasoned than their school and public library counterparts in supporting distance learners. Their insight and experience are valuable to new explorers of the medium.

We'll take a look at the needs of this new class of library users and how school and public libraries welcome distance learners and support their instructors. Then we'll see what can be learned from the academic library model.

WHO ARE THESE PEOPLE, ANYWAY?

The common characteristic among distance learners who become library users is that their needs surprise local library staff. They may be young adults or senior citizens. Their needs may be as simple as access to the library Internet connection or as complex as needing assistance in learning how to use hardware and software in order to make a presentation to the class.

In many circumstances, distance learners don't benefit from the environment created when faculty and librarians communicate about classroom projects in their school.

They may be strangers to information resources, lack research skills, or even be without a library card.

To get beyond these hurdles, library staff should rely on some traditional library sleuthing. If a distance learning student is having trouble expressing his or her needs, try asking questions like these:

- What course are you taking, and at what level?
- Do you have a course syllabus, or can we see one online?
- Is there a bibliography or Webliography for the class?
- Is there a resource person at your hosting site who could help us clarify your needs?

Once the groundwork is laid, a reference interview can reveal the learner's need more clearly, and the appropriate library services can be put into play.

Now let's look a little more closely at services that make distance education work effectively for students.

HIGH SCHOOL DISTANCE LEARNING PROGRAMS

High school distance learning programs function a little more informally than programs in higher education. "Students take courses online but are expected to do their research and assignments off-line," explained Connie Schlotterbeck, media specialist at Newton (Massachusetts) South High School, whose school participates in the Virtual High School (VHS) run by the Concord Consortium.

"VHS is structured so that students should do the online portion of the course at school, not at home. They receive the overview, expectations, syllabus, and feedback from the instructor online. Then the student pursues whatever avenues are necessary to complete the project or course. In our case, since the VHS connection is in our library, the students proceed directly to our resources (electronic periodicals, book collection, etc.) to continue their research" (Schlotterbeck, 2000).

A virtual high school's most consistent on-site staff person is a technical coordinator, someone who makes sure that students have access to the hardware and software they need to complete their coursework. That individual may be the only person in the school who has the inside track on what's expected of the student—and his or her job is not necessarily to facilitate learning. The results in terms of learner support are uneven at best.

The School Library Media Specialist's Role

Since media specialists are often charged with managing campus technology, it's not surprising that some school librarians are also distance learning site coordinators. Tom Anderson, media specialist at Oakmont Regional High School in Ashburnham, Massachusetts, is one. Tom commented, "I went to an information session on the VHS program a couple of years ago. A teacher here wanted to develop a course, so we got involved . . . We had to commit 20 percent of my time, and I went through an eight-week orientation. It took several hours a week. I learned about the role of a VHS site coordinator and solving technical problems. My role is to be an intermediary between students and teachers and the academic registration process" (Anderson, 2000).

Even when the school librarian is not also a site coordinator, chances are he or she will wind up troubleshooting technical difficulties for online learners. New distance learning programs typically have start-up problems, resulting in frustration for students working under pressure. "Having a good technical infrastructure is crucial. In the first year or two of the program, people had to have a very high tolerance for frustration" (2000), Tom noted. Once those problems are resolved, the library can focus on the business of supporting the learning, not the delivery system.

When one person assumes the responsibility for site coordination and the library media program, supporting the information needs of the distance learner is less challenging. If the librarian is not a distance learning site coordinator, advocacy for the student with the school's site coordinator becomes important. Access to course syllabuses and bibliographies makes the difference between being ready and being blindsided.

Kathy Somerville, Librarian at Hudson (Massachusetts) High School, a VHS site, warned, "We don't have much communication with our kids' distance learning teachers. We never see the syllabus, so we don't really have any knowledge of what's going on" (2000).

"Typically," she commented, "we hear about a project when we get oddball reference questions. We also have problems when teachers assign Web sites that our firewall blocks. If we knew about the sites and the course bibliography in advance, we'd be better prepared and the students would be less frustrated" (Somerville, 2000).

The problems are universal and familiar in the teacher-student context, traditional as well as online. Tenacity and diplomacy are called upon to improve the situation. Working closely with the program site coordinator makes a difference.

LIBRARY RESOURCES FOR DISTANCE LEARNERS

Because students who learn in a virtual classroom may never meet their instructors, local libraries can play a significant role. They may offer a home for the program hardware and software and troubleshoot both, provide traditional library resources, make unusual interlibrary loans, facilitate students' use of additional libraries, provide proctoring, and even promote the course offerings.

TRADITIONAL LIBRARY RESOURCES TO SUPPORT DISTANCE LEARNERS

Because distance learners aren't on campus where traditional resources are available, it's critical that they have the benefits of equitable resources. The Association of College & Research Libraries (ACRL) is very clear about the responsibilities that should be assumed by the originating institution, and we'll examine their recommendations later. Outside of the higher education forum, expectations are less consistent. As the local individual most concerned with a student's success, librarians may use all of the traditional resources. Included are:

- Orientations to online research
- Reference work
- Collection development
- Interlibrary loan
- Delivery
- Access to electronic databases, both remote and in the library

Let's take a closer look at orientations to online research and reference work, two traditional library services used untraditionally by distance learners.

Orientations to Online Research

An excellent student orientation to research is provided by Old Dominion University Libraries Distance Learning Services in Norfolk, Virginia. On a simply designed page, students are offered the opportunity to "Start Your Research Here." Following simple steps, the page links to:

- Select a Topic
- Find Background Material
- Find Books
- Find Articles
- Find Other Resources
- Evaluate Sources
- Use a Style Manual
- Ask for Help

Each page provides links to resources and some tips for using them, effectively migrating a live in-class orientation to an online one (Old Dominion University Library, 1999).

The Old Dominion model extracts the most important elements of student orientation and places them online so that anyone with a little time and patience can use them. Host libraries will need to define learning objectives for their own students and provide similar material and access.

In addition to the research process, students need orientation to specific library resources that are only a click away. Using traditional resources remotely may be unfamiliar. Providing answers to some frequently asked questions helps. Include information about the following services in your FAQ for distant learners:

- Remote access to databases
- Electronic access to interlibrary loan
- How materials can be delivered to distant students
- Reference service by e-mail or chat

Susan Lowe, assistant dean for Off-Campus Library Services, University of Maine System Network, pointed out that, "We provide initial training about using library material, what the University Network (UNET) is and what we do. Our staff develops lots of Interactive Television (ITV) instruction on information literacy. We see all syllabuses, and we always add an informational insert about resources. That's especially important with students who are out of state. We develop online tutorials to help those students prepare" (Lowe, 2000).

Reference Work

What becomes of the reference process when the librarian and information seeker are far apart? Can the integrity of the reference interview be maintained? The Multnomah County (Oregon) Library established an asynchronous online reference inquiry service. In doing so, the library helped to define the issues in delivering reference to remote learners. Some of the questions that hosting libraries will need to ask of remote enquirers are:

- What is the student's age or reading level?
- What sources has he or she checked?
- What are the breadth and sources of information the student needs?
- If expenses outside the library's budget are required to answer the question, what is the maximum the student can/will pay?

Probably the most challenging aspect of asynchronous reference is the difficulty in clarifying the reference request. Multiple e-mails may be required before a user and librarian have narrowed the topic to its true focus. If learner and librarian check mail only several times daily, the time needed to clarify questions and find answers is extended.

Putting reference online raises some additional questions about internal resources. Will staffing needs increase? Are additional technical resources required? How will the library limit its service to those in its service area? Is the library's collection adequate for the expanded subject inquiries?

Online reference can be delivered in real time by using chat or telephony. In that case, in addition to these ques-

Figure 3–1 More About Real-Time Online Reference Home Page

Have you ever dreamed of working from your living room? Real-time online reference work may be your fantasy job.

Many libraries that offer real-time chat reference provide it as an after-hours service. Their staff, rather than sitting in a darkened and closed library building, usually works from home.

Chat is a text-based synchronous way of communicating. Using chat, each party types messages into a split screen. Both participants see the two halves of the conversation emerge as they type.

Imagine sitting in your cozy den, cocoa in hand, when an audible signal lets you know there's an incoming reference request. You go to your computer, click an icon to accept a chat request, and the reference interview begins.

Surrounded by just a very few books (a good dictionary is many librarians' favorite), you play your online Public Access Catalogs (PAC), search engines, and full-text databases like a symphony.

You answer the user's question without ever rising from the desk. You have access to some good information, but books are required for a full answer. You reserve material for the customer at his or her local library so that he or she can pick it up in the morning.

In the near future, typing may go by the wayside. Already, specialized software enables the librarian and patron to see the same Web sites at the same time. Conveying voice over the Internet is a developing option for reference, but it requires that both parties have a microphone, the same software, and a speedy connection.

tions, the library must determine the technical requirements, service hours and how the caseload will be managed (see Figure 3–1).

There is a range of interactive class environments in higher education, but none tailored specifically for library reference. *24/7 Ref* is a pilot project of the Metropolitan Cooperative Library System administered by the California State Library. The goal of this project is "to provide libraries with the tools they need to do live reference on the Web" (Metropolitan Cooperative Library System, 2000). *24/7 Ref* began as a federally funded project by LSTA Resources. It uses a similar interactive approach to some online retailers, and according to the project Web site:

- Enables staff to track and capture details on the reference questions asked and answered.
- Provides scripting to prompt reference staff to ask certain questions for certain subjects, or refer to certain key sources, and allows easy authentication of the patrons so that only library card holders can query the staff or access any proprietary databases.
- Allows routing of calls, so staff could work in remote locations, such as networking a group of librarians from different libraries or staff working at home.
- Permits live, real-time collaborative browsing over the Web . . . (Metropolitan Cooperative Library System, 2000).

When resources such as *24/7 Ref* are affordable and accessible, real-time reference with remote users will become an important tool in library business for remote learners.

Collection Development

Students who are enrolled in courses not typically offered within a high school's walls pose some collection development challenges. Though most distance learning teachers are expected to provide access to all the materials their students will need, either through Web links or by mail, it doesn't always work that way. A student's investigations may lead him or her in new directions. In such cases, a school or public librarian may find himself or herself pushing to locate interlibrary loan material he or she has never needed before. If the course is a popular one, there may be budget implications and the need for collection development.

"I wasn't involved in developing the curriculum our students use," Connie Schlotterbeck said, "but so far we've had all the course requirements on hand. My library hasn't added resources yet to support the courses our students take, but I think we should plan on that as the program grows" (2000).

Sometimes specific resources are close at hand but not in the students' public or school library. In such cases, librarians may become intermediaries for students who need access to collections that may not normally be open to them. A call to a colleague in a special or academic collection will help to establish the legitimacy of the student's inquiry.

Adult students are often independent learners, visiting libraries of all sorts unannounced. Susan Farr, a student at the University of Rhode Island Graduate School of Library and Information Science, wrote, "I took cataloging and was helped enormously by the Worcester (Massachusetts) Public Library reference staff who lent me cataloging materials which were not part of the general collection and even gave me some insight into how some oddities might be classified. I also used both the Worcester Public Library and the Boston (Massachusetts) Public Library research library and reference section to finish course work in my reference class . . . In both places, staff bent over backwards to find the often-obscure sources I needed without actually doing my assignments for me (a fine line, sometimes)" (Farr, 2000).

In Susan's case, library staff extended extraordinary resources to enable a student to complete assignments. As the lines blur between the walls of academe and the public forum, librarians should be alert and responsive to non-traditional requests for resources.

NON-TRADITIONAL LIBRARY ROLES TO SUPPORT DISTANCE LEARNERS

Librarians have identified some brand-new ways in which they can support distance learners. Proctoring and marketing are two.

A proctor monitors the administration of a test. Though the educational trend has moved away from monitored skill and memory tests, there is still sometimes a need for timed and supervised examinations. "The library staff have proctored exams several times by request," said Ms. Owen Shuman, director of the Groton (Massachusetts) Public Library. "Because it takes little staff time and provides a needed service, we are happy to proctor exams. The instructor mails the exam to us and we make sure the student has a quiet place to work and starts and finishes on time. We mail the exam back to the instructor" (2000). The hosting facility may receive token remuneration from the educational organization. "The remuneration from one student was small but enjoyable—a bottle of wine" (2000). This simple service can be invaluable when it's needed.

In Texas, the growing need for proctoring led to the establishment of the Texas Computer-Based Testing Collaborative, a group of twenty-two colleges and five public libraries that have established testing centers to make test-taking more convenient for remote learners. Students show identification when they arrive to ensure that the person who takes the test is actually the student enrolled in the course. Testing is conducted in existing college or library facilities using testing software. Though the Texas collaborative is grant-funded, some colleges in a similar Illinois system charge a small fee—ten to fifteen dollars—to provide the service (Young, 2001).

Marketing courses are an unexpected undertaking for librarians. Yet Connie Schlotterbeck noted, "We need to get the word out better—kids get excited about what's being taught online. I make the effort to pull out the catalog and show them the possibilities. Sometimes that's all it takes" (2000). In fact there's no better advocate for distance learning programs than the librarian, who may host the program equipment, support the learners, and take an active interest in what's accomplished. By working closely with guidance counselors, librarians can open gateways to courses students never dreamed were available.

yourhomework.com™
An Innovative Approach for Excellence in Education!

We provide free services for teachers to post homework assignments for their students. Easily integrate assignments, teacher email, class web page, and homework help to harness the power of the web for your class.

Students/Parents
Teachers
Librarians
Homework Help
Calendar
Mall/Fundraiser
FAQ
Contact Us
About This Site

Teachers:
Post homework assignments on the Web
Send and receive Email
Design a home page for your class
Send Assignment Alerts to local libraries

Students:
View homework assignments on the Web
Turn in homework assignments on time
Communicate with your teacher
Show responsibility for your work

Parents:
Communicate with teachers
Monitor homework assignments
Stay informed of class progress
Participate in your child's education

Schools:
Ensure leading edge communication
Pay no administrative costs
Integrate technology into the curriculum
Improve faculty's technology skills

Libraries:
Receive automatic Assignment Alerts
Prepare for student research projects
Communicate effectively with teachers
Work with schools to improve services

PTA Fundraising:
Enjoy effortless fundraising year 'round
Eliminate solicitation by students
Receive cash quarterly
Requires no management by school

Figure 3–2: Teacher/Librarian Online Service: Yourhomework.com Home Page. Yourhomework.com name and logo are trademark of YOURHOMEWORK LLC. All screen shots, content, and graphic image reproductions used from yourhomework.com are copyrighted property of YOURHOMEWORK LLC.

Library Services for Distance Instructors

Has your library worked closely with a teacher in the community or school as he or she develops and teaches curriculum? Assisting the same teacher as he or she begins the distance teaching adventure will challenge and extend familiar boundaries. Some of the ways you may collaborate are by developing bibliographies, pathfinders or subject directories, providing custom class assignment pages, and reserving and delivering material.

Media specialists are partners in curriculum development for the traditional classroom and can be even more instrumental in the virtual setting. Expertise in identifying and evaluating resources can inform the evolution of course content whether it's by making literary connections or gathering interdisciplinary resources. Effective searching and skill in evaluating electronic resources are two of the important contributions librarians can make to teachers as they develop online curricula. Another is Web page development for class assignment pages on which resources can be gathered for easy access.

For younger students, managing homework may be an ongoing issue. A response to the ongoing challenge of keeping parents and librarians informed about kids' homework assignments was mounted by yourhomework.com (Yourhomework.com, LLC, 2000). The free service provides Web space and services for teachers to post homework assignments for their students (see Figure 3–2). Librarians can receive automatic assignment alerts and communicate with teachers through it. Developing such online communities for learning support holds promise for distance and traditional learning.

You may even be a resource person online, participating in real-time or asynchronous discussion about resources. Last but not least, you may find that you are supporting a teacher as student, introducing the resources on another level entirely.

Electronic Pathfinders and Other Resource Organizers

When a local teacher asks a librarian to orient students to library resources, he or she knows exactly what to do. He or she might highlight specific relevant print and electronic materials and assemble a small collection for use by the class. What if the students never set foot in the library?

Librarians have organized resources since libraries began, and the skill has transferred seamlessly to the Web in the form of subject directories. The *Librarian's Index to the Internet*, originally coordinated by Carole Leita, is a primary collection of evaluated, reviewed, and well-organized Web links.

Taking subject directories a step further, the Internet Public Library (IPL) created Pathfinders. "IPL Pathfinders are home-grown guides written by IPL staff which are intended to help you get started doing research on a particular topic, both online and at your local library" (Internet Public Library, 2000). Organized by general subject areas such as "Arts & Humanities" or "Health, Medicine & Nutrition," the Pathfinders are a growing collection of approximately 75 resource guides. Each includes general and Internet information and refers the reader to print titles available at local public libraries. The IPL Pathfinders are fairly generic, but can be used locally by librarians as models on which to build similar resources. If generating custom pathfinders is beyond the local ability, linking to IPL's Web site is an alternative.

Building custom pathfinders takes the resource to the next level. A good example of resources tailored to meet the needs of individual classes is Bowdoin College Library's *Course Guides*. For courses offered in current and past course catalogs, the library staff works with individual professors to build resource guides. Depending on the course content and structure, each may contain:

- Introduction to the course
- Information about using the library catalog

- General resources (including indexes and licensed databases)
- How to find reviews
- Links to related Web sites and scholarly papers
- Information on citing sources (Bowdoin College Library, 2000).

On each of the Bowdoin College Course Guides links to library orientation pages are prominent on each page, as is the contributing librarian's name.

Reserves and Delivery

The reserve shelf goes electronic when class participants are scattered. Depending on the structure of the hosting academic institution, the puzzle of getting reserved material to students takes on new dimension.

At the University of Maine, reserves and delivery are big business. The University includes seven remote sites and additionally serves students at one hundred locations statewide and many beyond state borders. Courses depend heavily on electronic reserves and delivery. Style manuals are the only materials placed in hard copy on reserve at the scattered locations.

"Asynchronous students," according to Susan Lowe, "request materials at a central site or campus for pick up, and they can expect to receive them within three days. Students' library cards get them into the databases we provide. If what they need isn't there, we'll mail documents to their home addresses at no charge within three days" (2000).

Reserves are built into the system as well. Susan said,

"We use electronic reserves extensively. We run special-ized reserve software and catalog online resources to be sure they are available" (2000). It becomes rapidly appar-ent that cataloging online resources becomes critically im-portant when students use resources remotely. If browsing the catalog is the primary method for students to discover information, Web resources must be thoroughly cataloged to be accessible.

Your Online Librarian

What happens to the student who lacks the information literacy or navigational skills to take advantage of online tutorials or subject guides? Earlier we examined using chat for reference. Another potential use for chat is to create the opportunity for library staff to help guide students through the information maze. In addition to chat refer-ence, the online librarian is ready to respond to general resource navigation questions. This value-added service pulls together all the resources described above by provid-ing office hours for library help. Some of the uses of di-rect interaction with students are less concrete than reference inquiries and may include:

- Helping students to build logical links between their questions and the available resources
- Referring students to resources outside the library's holdings
- Helping students to construct productive search strat-egies.

Clare Underwood, media specialist at Groton Dunstable

(Massachusetts) Regional Middle School, found that helping faculty members undertake their own distance learning called upon all of her skills. Clare wrote: "In some cases, the assistance has been fairly small, taking them through electronic resources that they can then access at here or at home. In others, I've 'walked' teachers through online registration and the transmission of class work to their teachers. We have also loaned library technology to these teachers (*after* having taught them to use it,—i.e., scanners, digital cameras, camcorders) to complete course work. One teacher laughingly told me that she felt like I was teaching her how to be her own librarian!" (Underwood, 2000).

Clare's experience is not unique. As adults and young people undertake the distance learning adventure in unsettled territory, their school and public librarians are accepting new roles. Let's take a look at some of the progress academic librarians have made toward setting standards for library roles in distance education and tackling tough issues like copyright and collaboration.

STANDARDS FOR DISTANCE LEARNING LIBRARY SERVICES

In 1998, the Association of College and Research Libraries (ACRL) revised 1990 guidelines to respond to the increase in non-traditional learning experiences and the numbers of unique environments in which they were offered. Included in the new *Standards for Distance Learning Library Services* philosophy are assumptions that:

- access to adequate library service is essential in post-secondary education regardless of where it's offered;
- traditional on-campus services cannot be stretched to accommodate distance learners;
- additional resources are required and should be provided by the institution that originates the education; and
- services for distance learning communities may be different but should be equivalent to those provided for on-campus learners (Association of College & Research Libraries, 1998).

Any library or school considering developing distance learning will find time reading the ACRL guidelines will be well spent. The guidelines clearly delineate the responsibility of the originating institution for managing the program so that a student never encounters obstacles to learning simply because he or she is learning remotely. Attention to the standards will reduce the students' frustration and the librarian's feeling of ambush from outside his or her library's walls.

COPYRIGHT

In the cut-and-paste world, copyright is a bigger problem than ever, both for faculty and students. Instruction about copyright and fair use has become a substantial portion of information literacy training in public and school library settings. It's just as big in the academic world. The reasons are twofold: acquiring permissions to use protected material on the Web is time consuming and it's expensive.

Susan Lowe of the University of Maine commented, "Probably the most demanding portion of our work is copyright. We spend a lot of time teaching faculty about fair use in the electronic environment. The faculty wants to use images behind their course content. We've been responsible for permissions, and it's been overwhelming. Now we have a request in place that faculty get their own permissions and pay fees from their departmental budgets. We also provide resources for the faculty—for example, we have public performance rights for a substantial list of videos. The list is posted. Technicians won't show a title unless it appears on the cleared list" (2000).

The UNET Faculty Service page states clearly: "Copyrighted materials that will be included in course packs or placed on reserve at the off-campus centers or sites must be copyright-cleared and renewed for every semester that they are used. For faculty teaching through the University Network, the Off-Campus Library office provides clearance services. Please submit requests ten weeks prior to the start of the semester to allow ample time for clearance" (University of Maine System Network for University and Technology Services, 2001).

Copyright clearance is an issue taken very seriously and one for which guidelines are still evolving. Old Dominion University Libraries respond to the complexity by providing an excellent *Copyright/Fair Use/Intellectual Property Bibliography* on its Web site (Old Dominion University Library, 2000).

COLLABORATION

To provide equitable and effective support for distance learners, librarians must build collaborations with other professionals in their buildings or communities. The academic experience once more provides a role model.

Susan Lowe asserted, "Our department is an important point of contact when faculty is designing courses. The site personnel aren't necessarily University employees, and we have to develop a relationship. We provide initial training about using library material, what UNET is and what we do. Our staff develops lots of ITV instruction on information literacy" (2000).

Within the context of an educational setting, the librarian may need to convince faculty members that materials outside of the standard collection development practice of the library should be purchased with departmental funds. In that case, building bridges of trust and support with the faculty is particularly important to the librarian. Being included in the institutional information loop may take commitment as well.

"I'm a systems librarian, and as an 'outsider'," commented Susan Lowe, "I have to work hard to get the cooperation of all the librarians in the system. They coordinate their services, and I attend all the library directors meetings. I participate in the circulation heads group and the database selection committee. That's the way to make things work" (2000).

CONCLUSION

School and public libraries have both traditional and new roles to play in supporting distance learners and instructors.

Some familiar roles that take on new dimension are reference, which may be delivered asynchronously or in real time; student orientation, which may be presented solely on the Web; and helping students to locate unique resources outside of the confines of the library's walls.

Some roles that are completely new are providing sites and technical support for distance learning programs, posting class assignments pages, advocating for new distance learning opportunities, and acting as an "online librarian."

Academic libraries have set a standard from which school and public librarians can learn. They clearly define the equity to which distance learners are entitled and the responsibility of the originating academic institution in establishing the necessary resources. Academic libraries have approached the complexities of copyright and collaborations effectively.

What's ahead for school and public libraries in support of distance learning? According to Connie Schlotterbeck, "The challenges of supporting kids who are distance learners are communication and staying aware of what's coming up. The reward is working with an exciting new technology with lots of potential. Kids can take courses our school doesn't offer and can learn about educational expectations in other parts of the country and even the world . . . We need to get the word out better—kids get excited about what's being taught online. It's creative and nontraditional" (2000).

REFERENCES

Anderson, Thomas. 2000. Telephone interview with Carolyn Noah, Ashburnham, Mass., November 25.

Association of College & Research Libraries. 1998. *Standards for Distance Learning Library Services* [Online]. Available: www.ala.org/acrl/guides/distlrng.html [10 November 2000].

Bowdoin College Library. 2000. *Course Guides* [Online]. Available: http://library.bowdoin.edu/classes/ [15 December 2000].

Farr, Susan. 2000. Telephone interview with Carolyn Noah, Sterling, Mass., November 20.

Internet Public Library. 2000. *Pathfinders* [Online]. Available: www.ipl.org/ref/QUE/PF/ [5 December 2000].

Lowe, Susan. 2000. Telephone interview with Carolyn Noah, Portland, Maine, November 25.

Metropolitan Cooperative Library System. 2000. *24/7 Reference Project* [Online]. Available: www.247ref.org [4 December 2000].

Old Dominion University Library. 1999. *Distance Learning Services* [Online]. Available: www.lib.odu.edu/services/disted/distedlhs.shtml [28 November 2000].

Old Dominion University Library. 2000. *Copyright/Fair Use/Intellectual Property Bibliography* [Online]. Available: www.lib.odu.edu/services/disted/copyrbib.html [4 December 2000].

Schlotterbeck, Connie. 2000. Telephone interview with Carolyn Noah, Newton, Mass., November 17.

Schuman, Owen. 2000. Telephone interview with Carolyn Noah, Groton, Mass., December 5.

Somerville, Kathy. 2000. Telephone interview with Carolyn Noah, Hudson, Mass, November 25.

Underwood, Clare. 2000. Telephone interview with Carolyn Noah, Portland, Maine, November 22.

University of Maine System Network for University and Technology Services. 2001. *Copyright and Broadcast Clearance* [Online]. Available: www.unet.maine.edu/Faculty_Services/Copyright.html [11 August 2001].

U.S. Department of Education, National Center for Education Statistics. 1999. *Distance Education at Postsecondary Education Institutions: 1997–98*. NCES 2000–013 by Laurie Lewis, Kyle Snow, Elizabeth Farris, Douglas Levin. Bernie Greene, project officer. Washington, D.C.: NCES.

Young, Jeffrey. 2001."Texas Colleges Collaborate to Offer Online Students Convenient Proctored Tests." *Chronicle of Higher Education* [Online]. Available: http://chronicle.com/free/2001/02/2001021501u.htm [16 February 2001].

Yourhomework.com, LLC. 2000. *Yourhomework.com* [Online]. Available: www.yourhomework.com/ [5 December 2000].

Chapter 4

Be Creative: Effective Distance Education Program Design

Even if you're a seasoned teacher or workshop leader, the first time you take familiar content and adapt it to the Web you'll likely experience an intense reevaluation of everything you know. In fact, what you'll do is examine course content with a whole new perspective. In the virtual classroom, just as in the traditional one, students benefit from a sense of community, the opportunity to interact with their peers and teacher, solid instructional content, and engaging learning activities. It's uncomplicated to mount paragraphs of text in the virtual classroom, but it's also not very stimulating. Creating effective distance learning experiences involves considerable planning. In many ways, developing distance learning is much like mounting a play, even to the extent that creators describe "mounting" or "putting up" both plays and Web sites.

BACKGROUND ISSUES

Because the development of distance learning demands organizational, human, and technical resources, start by examining the environment in which you operate. Some considerations are: the organization's goals in relationship to the project, the goals for your instructional offering, the availability of expertise, the project's potential audience, and technological demands.

The Organization

To initiate a distance education project places intense demands on staff time and financial resources. To build the case for committing the resources, make sure that you can tie the project closely to needs identified by your organization. If the relationship of your organization's mission, goals, and planning process to the distance learning project seems remote, think again. If an intrinsic function of your organization is to teach, you are already halfway there. Next, look for support in the organization's core planning documents. Did you build a strategic plan in which participants indicated a need for instruction delivered remotely? If not, is outreach part of the organization's mission? Either would be strong evidence that developing distance learning makes sense for you.

Once you have determined that the organization is supportive of your project, make sure that the parties involved have a clear sense of their roles and the time they may be called upon to contribute. In practical terms, block off dedicated project times regularly between the start and finish dates.

Objectives of the Instructional Offering

Before starting, articulate the learning objectives you've identified for participants in your distance learning opportunity. Some may be operational and others pedagogical. You may expect people to acquire a skill (such as mastering the electronic tools used in the course, developing Internet pathfinders, or cataloging library materials) or you may want them to grasp more abstract concepts.

The more clearly course goals are outlined the easier it will be to assess the success of the class when it's complete.

THE PLAYERS

The staffing structure of your organization, the monies available, and the time you have to give to the project might impact who is involved in the development of distance learning. The ideal distance learning project uses a team approach. The team includes participants with three types of expertise. They are a content expert, an instructional designer, and a Web designer or technical person. In addition, identify some students or potential students who are willing to help you test the outcome (Schrum, 1998). Choose your teammates with care, as you may find yourselves working under pressure and on deadline together. Personality, work style, and level of commitment to your project may become critical. You may do significant portions of your work asynchronously in the virtual environment, but consider planning as many as three team meetings to make sure all parties have the fullest communication. One will occur to brainstorm, a second as interactive lessons are readied to turn over to the technical designer, and a third to examine concerns identified by alpha testing as the project nears conclusion.

It's possible that the organization you work for cannot support the team approach and you might find that you are developing the distance learning experience primarily on your own. In this situation you'll need to fulfill each of the roles as outlined below. If you find yourself in this situation you might want to consider using courseware (for example, Blackboard or WebCT) instead of developing an entirely new Web interface from scratch.

This chapter looks at developing a distance learning experience from scratch, including content and design of a Web-based learning interface. If you are using a piece of courseware as the interface for your distance learning course, most of the team roles as outlined below still apply. The difference is in the role of the Web designer/technical specialist, a role that is minimized when you are using courseware. Even when using a software product for the interface, you still need to consider the organization of your content and how to use the interactive features of the software program (chat, discussion boards, surveys, and quizzes) to their best advantage.

For the purposes of this section of the chapter, let's assume that you are the content expert and the individual in charge of assembling the team. You'll also act as project referee, helping to resolve differences among the team.

The Content Expert

Your distance learning offering will be built on a foundation of information, so start with someone who has a mastery of the content. The content expert is not responsible for figuring out how best to make the transfer of the content from live classroom and print to the Web but he or she is responsible for knowing the topic and helping to determine how the transfer of the content to the Web format will work best.

Whether the distance learning experience is geared towards children, teens, or adults—whether the information to be delivered consists of concrete ideas or abstract concepts—make sure that the content is solid. Gather and review the resources needed to teach the class in the traditional setting. Update the content just as you would for classroom presentation. As you go through this process, remember that the immediacy of the Web puts extra pressure on providers to be current.

If you're not an experienced distance learner yourself, you may wish to enroll in a course available from online instructors like Element K, whose offerings primarily teach computer applications, to know what others are providing and to get an idea of how learning on the Web works. Many professional organizations, such as the American Association for School Librarians (AASL) or the Young Adult Library Services Association (YALSA) offer free distance learning opportunities to members. Search the Web to learn whether there are other models you can follow, especially ones that are closely related to your content. Identify what works well in terms of structure and interactivity, and recognize what doesn't.

Staying abreast of developments in Web programming languages and applications is a daunting task and specialized enough that it's unlikely the content developer will have keen familiarity with these issues. However, even a basic knowledge of HTML (HyperText Markup Language) serves the content specialist well in terms of understanding the potential and limitations of the Web environment and in communicating with other members of the team.

The amount of time consumed by developing and leading distance learning, especially for a beginner, is significantly greater than the commitment of developing a conventional course. Expect that it will ordinarily take two or three times longer than required for traditional preparation of the content (Wiesenberg and Hutton, 1996). The development of your first offering could take significantly longer. The time devoted to assembling a new Web site to provide structure for your offerings and the commitment may be as much as five times the traditional course development time.

Chapter 5 of this book is devoted to the distance learning educator, so read on for more details.

The Instructional Designer

Even if you have the content down cold, you'll probably need help making the transition to the Web. That's where the instructional designer comes in. The instructional designer may have little or no knowledge of the content you want to teach when you begin to work together. He or she *will* have an extensive understanding of pedagogy and how to adapt teaching technique to the new environment.

The instructional designer will probe for an overall sense of the course content, the most important information you need to convey, and the kinds of learning activities that have worked in teaching the content previously. You will remain in charge of the content, but the designer will help you to conceptualize the interactivity required to engage your learners. Expect this expert to work through many different possibilities before making a recommendation for the portion of your content most adaptable to interactivity. The outcome of your work with an instructional designer will be much like a play manuscript—including text, links to other internal or external information, ideas for the interactive components, and functional directions for the Web designer.

If you are using courseware you will work with the instructional designer in analyzing the capabilities of the software and how to best use interactive components available to create a successful student learning experience.

The Web Designer or Technical Expert

The Web designer brings insight to what's possible on the Web and is responsible for weaving the content and activities together into the finished product. (When using courseware the components are predetermined by the software vendor.)

Since the possibilities for interactivity expand constantly, this person is key to bringing your concepts to life. He or she should contribute a thorough understanding of Web functionality. It's likely that there's some programming experience in his or her resume. It may even be the case that one individual can provide programming and graphic design for your site, though it's less likely as Web applications become increasingly sophisticated.

However, he or she may subcontract with others to program the functionality described by the instructional designer and to create the look and feel of the site you develop together. Depending upon the demands of the site you create, the Web designer may work with a variety of other professionals, such as a media producer, graphic designer, and a "techie," or hardware/software specialist. When you hire a Web designer who subcontracts with others, he or she becomes a project manager.

In a very real sense, the Web designer is the producer of your distance learning project. Working within the parameters you've defined for completion, he or she will develop a timetable for the creation of each piece of your site.

Student Testers

Some projects have the luxury of involving students in conceptual and pedagogical design from the outset. Many don't. At the least, recruit a few students who are willing to suffer with you through numerous versions of the site and activities as they evolve. In designing distance education you may find that familiarity with the content will be a handicap, causing you to make assumptions or logical leaps that are unavailable to others. Insight from a member of your potential audience will be valuable as you fine-tune. As in theater, the reviews have a lot to do with an effort's success or failure.

POTENTIAL AUDIENCE

Some characteristics of your project's desired audience should be considered in advance. There may be course prerequisites, or students may be drawn from a class of employees. For example, the students for "BLT to Go," a basic library techniques course in administration, were primarily drawn from a group of individuals who were paraprofessional public library directors in small communities. It was assumed that the group had some common understandings about libraries.

Making assumptions about their technical savvy, however, was counterproductive. The course providers knew that each library and staff member had access to a PC connected to the Internet and significant amounts of Internet and application training. Not anticipated was the huge variation in the ability of participants to use simple browser commands to print, navigate, select, and save.

Such miscalculations can impair the effectiveness of a learning experience. Solutions such as advanced skill inventories and preparatory hands-on training can repair these handicaps, but early assessment is critical. Also important is an evaluation of the level of equipment and technology available to students and making sure that students know what technology is required before registering for the course.

It takes much more than mouse skills to define the best candidate for distance learning. To learn more about those skills, read Chapter 6.

TECHNICAL CONSIDERATIONS

Before you can begin to design any course components, seriously consider technical capabilities, both at your end and the student's. If your offering will include any interactivity or media—in fact, any component besides simple text—you need to assess both carefully.

Try to identify the lowest common denominator in technical resources among your potential students and design for them. Will people participate from slow home connections or on old machines? Small, or thumbnail, graphics download reasonably quickly. Activities based on HTML with minimal graphics also load well. However the video, audio, and movies that thrill a user require lots of bandwidth and will only frustrate someone with a slow connection. For example, a megabyte of data (pictures, sound, or text) downloads in 4 minutes and 38 seconds on a 28.8 telephone modem, but only 1.8 seconds on a T3 line at 45 bps (Jacob, 1997). It will play in less than one minute, so the return value may be scanty. Video is best reserved to relay information that requires broad movement; don't be tempted by talking heads!

Further, if you find that your potential users have old machines with limited disk capacity, they may not be able to stretch their memory resources to accommodate the range of plug-in applications they would need to enjoy high-tech accouterments.

Those who work in the electronic environment take e-mail for granted. E-mail is a critical way to communicate with participants in your distance learning offering. Students may need to participate in e-mail discussions and to receive updates and assignments by mail. However, don't assume that everyone who registers will have access to e-mail. Make e-mail a prerequisite, and make sure someone is available to help students sign up for a free e-mail service if necessary. In general, someone needs to be available for students to contact in order to troubleshoot the myriad technical difficulties they might encounter.

Finally, consider the students' technical abilities. You may need to make special accommodations to ensure their comfort level. Some of these accommodations are described below; others are presented in Chapter 6.

The other factors impacting technical choices are those on the provider's side. Based on your budget and on-site availability of technical assistance, you will make important decisions. They might include determining the best platform on which to run the site, depending upon who you expect to maintain it, or where it will actually be plugged into the Internet. You'll also need to decide if the course will reside in a directory in your organization's existing Web server or whether you'll purchase a domain name to identify your site. (If using courseware, the software vendor makes these decisions for you.)

If you have a fast local connection the site might reside on a server in your space. If not, it may be co-hosted by an Internet service provider (ISP). If that's the case, be sure to determine the level of technical support the ISP offers, when the office is actually staffed, and the hours during which your server will be physically accessible if necessary.

CHARTING THE COURSE

Now the fun begins! Your team is assembled, you know your audience's technical abilities and resources, and you've made some decisions about your own technical capabilities. You're ready to start charting the course. The effort demands the creativity of all parties involved and includes: brainstorming, developing a schematic design, crafting a timeline, designing interactivity, and determining the site's look, feel, and structure.

Brainstorming

The first team meeting should be a wide-open exploration of the educational and philosophical issues inherent in your course material. As content specialist, you should come prepared with a well-developed outline or syllabus defining your content and goals. Some of the questions the team should answer together are:

- What are the most important things you expect students to learn?
- How do students in a traditional setting learn the material best?
- Will online material complement or take the place of material delivered in a classroom?
- If you develop online material to complement the classroom experience, how will you select it?
- If you develop online material to complement the classroom experience, what material is best delivered in person?
- What material can be distilled to its essence without losing clarity, making it adaptable to the Web?

Usually the more concrete or skill-oriented a topic is the more easily adaptable it is to Web interactivity. Abstract content in a Web environment often works best through online discussion boards or chat conversations. If you choose to have traditional sessions, begin by reserving the

Figure 4–1: Web Interactivity Options for Turning "Live" Classroom Experiences into Successful Distance Learning.	
"Live" Classroom Model	**Distance Learning Possibilities**
Full class discussions	Audio, chat, discussion board
Small group discussions	Audio chat, discussion board
Lecture	Audio, chat, downloadable text files, video, PowerPoint presentations
Guest speakers	Audio, chat, discussion board, video
Homework assignments	Interactive components in which students take part in an activity online, downloadable lessons, Web quests
Research assignments	Web quests
Student presentations	Student Web pages, PowerPoint presentations, downloadable text files, audio
Quizzes	Interactive quizzes scored with instant instructor text or audio feedback and scoring
Syllabus	Downloadable text files or printed manual, Web pages or sections for each topic area

more theoretical or philosophical issues for discussion in person. Material that requires verbal or expressive nuance is also more effectively understood in person. If you are not able to include in-person meetings, try to determine the best way to get across minute details and abstract concepts in the online environment.

Web interactivity, nonetheless, can take a wide variety of forms. Choices range from traditional quizzes and game boards to online discussions through chat or topic boards (see Figure 4–1). Animation can be programmed to demonstrate cause and effect so that the learner's choices have a visible impact on what he or she sees on the screen. Audio clips can be used as discussion starters or the focus for demonstrations. Conferencing software can enable real-time interaction. Despite the dazzling array of options, thoughtful design will prioritize interactivity for the learning experience, make best use of the technology, and economize the time and electronic resources of the user. In other words, flashy programming for its own sake is counterproductive. Design simply and test your concepts on learners.

Interactivity serves another, equally important purpose aside from engaging students in learning activities. It can and should contribute to the development of the community of learners. As the course is built, be sure to include points along the way for shared learning and group discussion. Topic boards, discussion lists, chat, or newsgroups all can provide critical opportunities for students to support one another. However, the group leader must also take a proactive role in engaging active participation. Read more about this role in Chapters 5 and 6.

After you've identified the most important learning goals and brainstormed activities to support them, the team will go their separate ways. While there may be a significant period of time between the brainstorming meeting and the next gathering, there's plenty of work to accomplish in the meantime. Every player has a distinct role as well as distinct tasks. Further, it's critical to maintain good communication among all parties so that work can progress efficiently and collaboratively. One effective tool is a table indicating the components to be developed, who is responsible for them, and when they are to be delivered. A sample planning table is included in Figure 4–2. Another goal should be to establish an electronic discussion list so that everyone is party to all information exchanges.

Design Process

Both the technical and instructional designers use the information you've generated in your team meeting as raw material. The next phase of the project is intensely busy and stimulating. Because the steps described below are in logical, not exact chronological sequence, a typical master schedule is included to provide a sense of the project's sequence (see Figure 4–3). Many different elements of project development occur simultaneously, and the challenge is to bring the pieces together in a timely and harmonious way.

TECHNICAL DESIGN

If you are not using courseware to produce your distance learning experience, the Web designer's work begins where your first team meeting ends. Expect your technical expert to provide insight into the binding of content with technology, but remember that you are in charge. As team leader, you approve each increment of technical development. Be as clear as possible about your expectations and be sure that all of your understandings are agreed upon in writing. Record and initial any modifications you make along the way. Documents that determine the design, function, and look and feel of your site should be read and

Figure 4–2: Distance Learning Planning Table.

Content	Date written/ who	Date produced/ who	Date integrated/ who	Notes/ Questions
Course home page				
Welcome page text				
Course outline				
Overview text				
Chapter 1:				
Intro paragraph				
Chapter outline				
describe in-class, Web content				
Main content				
text				
related documents				
links				
Related activity description w/link				
Chapter 2:				
Intro paragraph				
Chapter outline				

Figure 4–2: Distance Learning Planning Table (con't).

describe in-class, Web content	
Main Content	
text	
related documents	
links	
Related activity description w/link	
Course calendar Description, detail assignments and expectations	
Course Contacts Description, course w/mailtos	
Resources Intro	Lists all the links, documents, discussion boards, and activities included in the course
Documents	
calendar	
Web links	
activities	
topic boards	

Figure 4–3: Distance Learning Master Schedule.

FEBRUARY

Team Meeting	2/21

Design
- Determine feature
  Set — 2/21
  Walk through — 2/28
- Final schematics — 2/28

Production
- Draft technical design — 2/28

Content
- Final syllabus — 2/21
- Final content — 2/28
  specifications
- Chapter 1 draft — 2/28

MARCH

Design
- Preliminary comps — 3/10

Team Meeting	3/24

Production
- Site skeleton — 3/24
- Discussion boards

Content
- Delivery of chapters — 3/24
- Delivery of activities
- Delivery of video scripts

APRIL

Design
- Final "look and feel" — 4/1

Team Meeting	4/21

Production
- Audio/video production — 4/7
- Alpha site — 4/14
- Discussion boards work — 4/14
- Content integrated — 4/21
- Beta site — 4/28

Content
- Delivery of exhibits — 4/7
- Bibliography
- Web links
- Case studies
- Final editing — 4/28

MAY

Production
- Bug fixes to final — 5/7

Content
- Bug fixes to final — 5/7

Live	**5/28**

discussed with all team members before agreement is reached.

First, the feature set will be locked in. The designer will create a flowchart to sketch the structure of the Web site. A sample flowchart is included in Figure 4–4. It describes the top-level relationships of types of page content to one

Figure 4–4: Sample Project Flowchart Showing the Basic Structure of a Course Web Site Design.

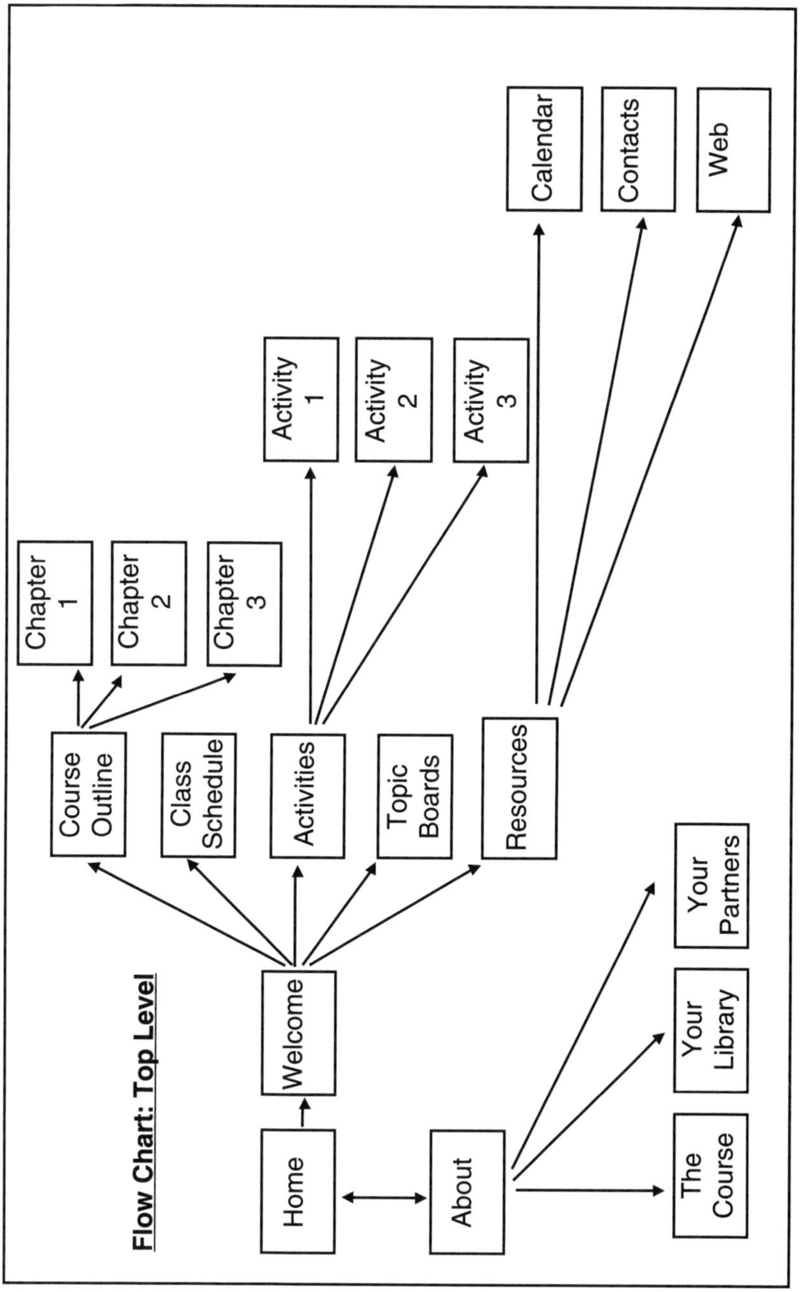

Figure 4–5: Sample Project Schematic Showing Course Information and How It Will Be Organized on a Course Page.	
⬍⬌	**Chapter I:** **The Public Relations Toolkit**
Outline Calendar Resources Activities Topic Boards Contacts	• Introduction: Why PR is important • Presentations and Working with the Media • Related Documents • Links • Activities

another. For example, it will indicate the relationships among the entry page, the content pages, and activities. Looking at the flowchart is like looking down on a stage blocked for a play, allowing you to anticipate the movement without giving a sense of the content.

From the flowchart evolves the schematic design. The schematic design provides a virtual marker for each type of content, and a separate page indicates each content type. The schematic begins to generally flesh out the content type, but at this point the pages provide only dummy text. For example, your group may have identified public relations as one important subject area. One page of the schematic will be a place holder for the Web site section on public relations. It will outline the types of information you expect will be included, for example text and quotations, links to activities and resources, and supplementary material on public relations. A sample page of a schematic design is included in Figure 4–5. Each content area will be outlined with a similar page. Together they provide a larger sense of how the site will be defined.

The walkthrough comes next and raises the ideas developed in the flowchart and the schematic design to the next level. For the walkthrough the Web designer takes the ideas expressed so far and mocks them up into very simple Web pages. These pages will not include real content but they will include links. Team members have the chance to move between the pages of the site, seeing how the flow from page to page and section to section works, and getting an idea of the feel of the design and the content.

A *comp*, or composite image, is developed next. The comp defines the look and feel of the site. During this phase of planning, the Web designer produces several different draft main pages and a sample of an internal page. The color schemes, layout, and fonts may vary widely. At this point your team must decide which style best suits your audience and content. You can pick and choose from characteristics you see in the comps, but if the Web designer has listened well, you'll probably see something you like from the beginning.

Consulting with the Web designer is not all that's occupying your time at this point. While the site is evolving technically, the educational activities are under construction as well.

INSTRUCTIONAL DESIGN

During your initial team meeting you've no doubt tossed around more ideas for online lessons than you can possibly use in your virtual classroom. Dialog between the tech-

nical and instructional designer clarifies the alignment between good pedagogy and potential applications of the
technology. The instructional designer will be especially
interested to know what interactive tools are available in
the technical specialist's portfolio. (If you are using
courseware, you'll want to look closely at the interactive
features available in the product you are using.) The instructional designer leaves with a bristling mental briefcase
of possibilities, and probably lots of notes. Armed with
basic knowledge of course content, he or she brings knowledge of effective learning environments to bear and begins
to make some choices.

You'll be in close contact with the educational consultant as he or she refines the most promising of the ideas
generated. There will be questions about the content, the
availability of informational resources, and your priorities
for learners. An activity, or lesson, may be fun to develop,
but if it's remote from the core of the content, it's not
worth pursuing. After lots of discussion, the consultant will
generate a list of possible lessons, many with interactive
components, and you'll be in the position of having to
choose from among them. Here are some considerations
for interactive components:

- Are they interesting?
- Are they central to the learning objectives of the
  course?
- Does the interactivity engage learners' attention?
- How long will each component take to complete? Is
  it a reasonable amount of time for learners to commit?

Testing lessons to determine how long they take to complete is critical. As with any in-class course, a distance learning instructor should have a realistic sense of the amount of time students will require to complete a lesson. While lessons are under development, test them with your student testers to see how long they take and whether they fit within the framework you've defined. If they're too long or demanding, rethink or revise the lessons.

Once you've narrowed the field to a manageable number of lessons, the educational designer will begin scripting. The lesson scripts are fluid documents. Your educational specialist knows how people learn best, but you know the content. Expect plenty of checking back from the educational specialist for information, facts, and insight into your user group. Also anticipate plenty of revisions in the flow of the activities. As team leader, you should expect to sign off on lessons as they are delivered, so be very clear about what you think works and what doesn't.

When the lessons are fully developed, they will be pages of script with annotations that look much like stage directions. The annotations describe the Web functionality of the lesson and provide a blueprint for the Web designer's work.

A sample script is presented in Figure 4–6. The sample script is a press release activity designed to follow live and online instruction about public relations and writing press releases. It is adapted from a Basic Library Techniques Administration course provided by the Central Massachusetts Regional Library System.

> **Figure 4–6: Sample Activity Script Showing the Instructional Designer's Text that Will Enable the Project Web Designer to Create the Activity.**

NEWS RELEASE ACTIVITY

Now that you've read about effective press releases, test your skills. The following press release is missing a number of critical elements. See if you can spot what's missing and where you would make changes.

NEWS RELEASE

Contact: Stephen Dedalus

For Release: Immediately

LIBRARY HOSTS LITERARY CENSORSHIP EVENT

Sunday evening the Deweyville Public Library presents Buck Mulligan of the Classic Theater in a dramatic reading from James Joyce's *Ulysses*. *Ulysses* is a 20th century classic once banned in the United States. The reading will be followed by a panel discussion.

Panelists are Professor Magennis of the English Department at Trinity College, Martin Cunningham, attorney, and Massachusetts State Senator Leopold Bloom.

The event is scheduled at 7:30 p.m. at the Deweyville Public Library. It is free and open to the public.

This is one of a series of events dealing with censorship. It is provided in conjunction with the "Banned Books" exhibit, which is open to the public during library hours during the month of September.

END

Now, take a look below at an improved version of the press release. Click on the changed text to see what important information has been added and why. How many did you get right?

Figure 4–6: *Continued*

NEWS RELEASE

Contact: Stephen Dedalus, telephone: 555–1234 *

Date: September 12, 2000 *

For Release: Immediately

LIBRARY HOSTS LITERARY CENSORSHIP EVENT

Sunday evening, September 17*, 2000, at 7:30 p.m.*, the Deweyville Public Library will present Buck Mulligan of the Classic Theater in a dramatic reading from James Joyce's *Ulysses*. *Ulysses* is a 20th century classic once banned in the United States. The reading will be followed by a panel discussion.

Panelists are Bernard Magennis, PhD,* of Trinity College's English Department, Martin Cunningham, Esq., of Cunningham and Conger, Attorneys at Law,* and The Honorable Leopold Bloom, of the Massachusetts State Senate.*

The event is free and open to the public. This is one of a series of events dealing with censorship. It is provided in conjunction with the "Banned Books" exhibit, which is open to the public during library hours during the month of September.

END

NOTES FOR WEB DESIGNER:

When student clicks on starred information, new screen pops up to show what's been identified. Students should be cued to close each new window before proceeding.

In sequential order, the notes are:

*You have found the event date.

*You have identified the program contact phone number.

*You have identified the release date.

*You have identified the program time, which should appear in the first line of a release.

*You have found a corrected speaker reference.

*You have found a corrected speaker reference.

*You have found a corrected speaker reference.

Content Development

Now the Web and instructional designers are your best friends, or at least they should be. Somewhere between your consultations with them, your responsibilities as content developer require your attention as well.

As you begin to write, consider the tone you'll take with the content. Will it be formal or conversational? Hip or traditional? These are also decisions that may also be reflected by the Web design. You will consult with your Web designer and decide early in the process what your organizational structure will be, as it may be reflected in the navigational design of the site. Once that's determined, you will write the text.

No matter the tone you choose, you should conclude with a readable Web content document. Because text on the Web has a very terse, bulleted aspect, it must be clear and logical. Transitions between lessons are particularly important and can be nearly invisible until you begin to put all the pieces together. The result of your labors will be a script for the content of the entire site, and if the site is large, this script can be a book in itself.

If the course you're developing for the Web began in a traditional setting and you have a syllabus, you're ahead of the game. You should be able to use it to chart the course to the new offering. (Chapter 5 provides detail on how to rework a syllabus from a document used in a live classroom to one used in online instruction.) In the hyperlinked environment, information requires careful and parallel structure or the learner may become lost in an information maze. Think of the distance learning offering in terms of its structure. Can you identify portions that will occur in every section or chapter? For example, the

---

Figure 4–7: Sample Permission Letter to Reprint Copyrighted Content.

888 Visual Literacy Drive
Anytown, MA

November 29, 2000

Ms. Jane Doe
Permissions Department
ABCD Press
468 Broadway
New York, New York 10021

Dear Ms. Doe:

This is to request your permission to reprint the chart published on page 56 of your publication Visual Literacy for All (ISBN: 0–122–12332–1).

I am requesting the permission to reproduce the chart in a Web-based presentation that will be mounted on my organization's Web site at: http://www.vislit.org.

Appropriate credit will be given on the site. It is anticipated that 25 students will access the material annually. The site will be accessible free of charge to authenticated learners only.

I have enclosed two copies of a release form. If my request meets your approval, please sign and return one. Please feel free to contact me with questions at 800–555–1111. I'd appreciate your response by January 15, 2001.

Sincerely,

Annie Content

Content Planning Guide (see Figure 4–2) was developed for a course that provided "Chapters" with parallel structure, including:

Figure 4–8: Sample Permission Form to Reprint Copyrighted Content.

Permission to Reprint

I grant permission to [author's name] to use the following material:

The material will be published on the [your organization] Web site at: [url].

We require that the following credit line be included:

I am authorized to grant this permission.

Signature

Print name

Title

Contact information

Date

- Intro paragraph
- Chapter outline
- Text narrative, sound, or images
- Related printable documents
- External links
- Descriptions of related lessons with links to them

Whether material is published online or in hard copy, be sure to observe fair use guidelines. Permissions will be required if you wish to use a significant portion of someone else's work. You may wish to develop a permissions request letter as well as a "Permission to Reprint" form on which content owners can indicate their willingness to have their work reprinted on your site. An example is given in Figures 4–7 and 4–8. Even if you use only a small portion of someone else's work, it's good practice to acknowledge the author in your credits.

You'll find as your work evolves that you revisit the same text more than once. Number and date your versions to make sure you can identify the most recent ones. A convention observed in the technical world is to use decimal numbers, for example version 1.1, 1.2, and so on.

PUTTING THE PIECES TOGETHER

By now you may feel like a juggler with the pieces of your Web site suspended in the air. When the instructional designer, Web designer, and content developer have completed their independent work and the team leader has approved it, it's time to shape the disparate pieces into a Web site. The Web content document with links clearly indicated, activity scripts with interactivity descriptions, and any additional support pages are turned over to the Web designer.

This transition offers a fine moment for a team meeting, virtual or live. The Web developer may have questions about the functionality envisioned for the lessons. He or she may offer constructive suggestions for modifications.

Building Courses on a Shoestring

The process outlined in this chapter describes an ideal scenario. An institution with ample resources, both financial and technological, can build a polished and refined product. What about those with the ambition to provide a distance learning experience but limited resources to devote to it?

Here's a barebones checklist to cover the bases in a much more economical, if less flexible way. It assumes that one person is the content provider and project manager.

- Determine the goals for the course(s) you will offer.

- Assemble a design team of two including the content provider and someone with basic technical expertise, including Web site management and HTML.

- Determine the features you want to include in the course—chat, threaded discussion, etc.

- Evaluate and select off-the-shelf courseware that provides the features you require.

- Write the course content.

- Ask someone you trust to review it for clarity and structure.

- Once you have fit the content into the courseware template, find some beta testers—people who may not necessarily know the content but will give you an honest assessment of the site's functionality.

- Make changes based on what the testers tell you. Then test again.

- Roll out the course.

- Be sure to get input from the learners—it will be invaluable when you are ready to revise.

The opportunity for everyone to share understandings about the direction for the work can prevent misunderstandings later. In theatrical terms, this is an opportunity for the whole cast to participate in a read-through.

The technical staff goes into production, fitting the content into the structure you have developed together. The interactivity will be programmed and ideas on paper become living, engaging Web pages. As the site is constructed, you'll have a couple of opportunities to see and test it.

The alpha site can be compared to a technical rehearsal, in which the crew responsible for the light and sound begin to demonstrate their magic. The site is in draft form, and though the functionality is in place, the work in progress is somewhat rough. Content may still be missing. The alpha test is the last time you can make any significant changes to the site. It offers another juncture at which a virtual or live team meeting may be helpful in order to be sure that what you're seeing lives up to everyone's expectations.

Though a professional Web designer will test the pages and interactivity across platforms, it's well advised for the team leader to double-check both. Remember to make sure that the Web pages work not only on different platforms but also on different browsers and with different browser versions. Keep a log called a "bug report" to provide the technical people with updates on problems you identify. Call on your potential student group to test the functionality with you.

The beta site, arriving some weeks later, is a fully equipped dress rehearsal. Content is in place and the functionality is complete. The site is almost ready to be publicly released. The beta phase is another moment to call in student testers. They'll provide you with the insight you need to make final adjustments. After those adjustments the site moves to final, when it is delivered to your site and care.

Once that's done, expect to receive project documentation. The documentation will include all the developmental pieces that went into your site, most of which will be very familiar. New and important is information about the files that have been delivered to you, including their names, functions, and basic information you will need if you have to modify them. While the end is in sight now, don't pay the final bills until you have documentation in hand.

As soon as you catch your breath, you can unveil your site.

GOING LIVE

The teaching staff is poised; the site is polished. What's left? You need to respond to the learners' technical needs. Some of the considerations include:

- Is technical support available for students who encounter mountainous obstacles in downloading, printing, or navigating? Do they understand the functionality of the site? A basic introduction to browser or mouse functions may be in order if they do not.
- Are FAQs provided to give access to answers to easily anticipated problems? Sometimes simple functions like printing from a document cause frustration.
- Is there a way for students to track their pathways

through the site? Checklists are a simple solution. Databases that require passwords and logins can also record student responses.

As you begin, engage learners in an assessment of their understandings of the course content and the success of the online learning experience. To structure the evaluation, refer to the learning objectives you established at the beginning of the course's development. The objectives should describe what students are expected to accomplish. Conduct a pre-assessment, which can be as informal as a group discussion or a written survey, to determine students' prior knowledge.

The assessment might include the participation of an outside evaluator who will conduct focus groups and maintain communication with learners as they go along. At the conclusion of the course, survey the students to determine what they learned. Compare the information from the pre-assessment and this post-assessment, along with what you expected students to learn, to determine the success of the course. With the outcome of the evaluation, you can incorporate their input into revisions for the next course offering. Crafting effective distance learning opportunities requires that you retool, revise, and go again.

Between the pre-assessment and post-assessment, of course, the most visible portion of your labor as instructor takes place. Chapter 5 provides insight into what's required of a distance learning instructor. That said, there is a range of lessons to be learned, hopefully vicariously, that can make your distance learning debut a manageable experience.

BARRIERS TO SUCCESS

No matter how thoughtful the approach, there are potential barriers to developing a successful distance learning course. These include language differences between team members, communication styles, consistency, time and space, work styles, and content fluidity. There's no guarantee that pitfalls can be avoided, but a little advance knowledge goes a long way. Read on for some advisory notices.

Language Differences

Language differences normally refer to commonly spoken tongues—for example, French, Spanish, English, or Arabic. In this case, the difference is between technical language and your own. A team leader doesn't *have* to know programming languages such as HTML or Java, but it helps. If your team includes a Web developer and subcontractors, be assured that at some point they'll toss around mysterious terms that are absolutely relevant to your objectives. For example, the terms used may describe functionality that your site needs. The best-case scenario is that you will witness an instance of technical snobbery, in which the developers are demonstrating they know more than you do. The worst-case scenario is that you may agree to something in the belief that you understand—and be wrong. In either case, it's helpful to have at least a working knowledge of Web programming capabilities. A basic understanding of what can and can't be accomplished on the Web and whether or not you can personally accomplish it makes you a much stronger advocate for your project.

Communication

Communication is critical as the project develops. By developing shared understandings, the team can reduce friction and move the project along more smoothly. Here are some guidelines to consider:

- Plan on at least three team meetings during the course of the project. The meetings will enable you to brainstorm, to review the proposed lessons for functionality, and to examine the alpha site together. In addition, schedule at least weekly telephone conversations with each of your teammates as the project develops. That way, everyone will understand how the work is developing and what requires immediate attention
- Take notes on the outcome of your meetings and share them with everyone concerned. Written notes provide documentation of group expectations if any one veers off course. They can be handy reminders of commitments that are made informally.
- Don't be afraid to repeat your understandings. In conversation, attention drifts. If you recapitulate your expectations, it's more likely that everyone will follow through.
- Set up an electronic discussion list. Share the written notes electronically with anyone who is involved.
- Be willing to appear uninformed. Ask that words you don't understand be repeated or defined. People tend

to try to understand words by their contexts, but that skill can be dangerous in this situation. Assert your need to know.

Work Style Challenges

Be assured that if there are four people working on your project, there will be four different work styles involved. Whether members tackle projects with gusto or laissez-faire, the project will get done only as quickly as the slowest contributor. This may appear to be an impenetrable obstacle, as changing someone else's work style is unlikely.

What you can do, however, is set a schedule. Designate delivery dates for individual components of the project. Make sure that you share common assumptions. Check back with each team member to learn about progress. Nudge, cajole, or flatter as necessary.

When in doubt, some team leaders up the ante. One approach is to build late delivery penalties into your contractors' agreements. Though it's an incentive, it's a negative incentive and may initiate a project with poor relations. Some team leaders take another, more subtle approach, and set delivery deadlines weeks ahead of the actual drop-dead date. In any case, the lack of control you ultimately exercise over the project may be a legitimate frustration.

Along with varying work styles, it's guaranteed that team members have varying temperaments. Count on occasional ego clashes as everyone becomes invested in the work. It's the team leader's job to focus the group's energy, redirect activity, and sometimes smooth feathers.

Time and Space

Time and space, virtual and real, can be terrible adversaries. In this context, time has multiple meanings. Most obvious is the staff time that must be invested to develop a course, ranging from twice to five times the normal development time.

Less obvious is the asynchronous nature of communication among the development team. If three meetings are planned, work that takes place between them is done offline and probably asynchronously. The joy of e-mail is that it can be sent or retrieved anytime. The frustration of e-mail is that there may be lags between exchanges. It's easy to become impatient or stew about outcomes. Thoughtful communication becomes even more important when every word is committed to print. (Anyone who has hit the "send" button too hastily while composing e-mail knows that a message is impossible to recapture.) It's worthwhile to find a rhythm of writing and reporting that works for you. Agree informally about your shared expectations for replies.

The limitations of space or geographical location can be surprising if a development team is spread out over a continent. It's tempting to assume that it really *doesn't* matter where people live in the electronic environment. It's not true. If the content development team is on one coast and the Web development is on another, a three hour time difference means that there's a very brief window of time on any given business day when all hands are on deck. Space, therefore, is a factor to consider in identifying team members.

Fluidity: Are We There Yet?

One of the Web's great strengths is that in contrast to print publishing, online documents are easy to modify. Don't like the way it looks today? Change it! You may never be truly finished.

It's all too easy to get stuck in a cycle of endless revision. Set a drop-dead date well in advance of the beginning of the online course. Stop meddling with the Web site after you've had input from testers. Then run the course, note student evaluations, and revise before running the class again.

OUTCOMES FOR FIRST-TIME DISTANCE LEARNING PROVIDERS

During the development process, you will spend ample time reflecting on learning outcomes for students. Not suprisingly, for the first-time developer, there's a remarkable process of discovery. Some of the lessons learned are to organize information consistently, to break course content into discrete portions, and to think in terms of Web functionality.

Consistency of structure is imperative. If outlining wasn't an approach you took to while writing course content for traditional presentation, it will no doubt become an important part of your online toolkit. Because of the hierarchical organization of Web information and the ease with which learners can lose their way in the absence of clear structure, outlines are the best way to make sure that pages follow parallel construction.

Small segments of text are easiest to comprehend online. For writers accustomed to the narrative style, it can be challenging to restructure ideas for Web content. Learners have trouble reading extensive text on the Web, so it's important to think small. Writers for distance learning learn to identify the smallest discrete sections of information and think of each as a Web page. The virtue of the Web, of course, is that the page doesn't stand alone even if a single page is brief. It can be linked to a wide array of other pages, resources, or lessons.

Learning to think in terms of Web functionality is probably the most interesting of outcomes for new developers. From the course outline, extracting the potential for interactivity means identifying the most engaging of content and cross-checking it mentally for its potential as a quiz, game, or discussion point.

CONCLUSION

Plenty of planning goes into developing distance learning opportunities. Included are assessments of the organization's abilities, resources, and commitment. The potential audience must be considered, and some determinations about the availability of technology must be made. Expertise in content, instructional design, and Web development must be recruited. Potential audience members can contribute insight as testers.

As a project begins, the development team brainstorms and determines timelines. Each player works independently and with the team to develop the project Web interface, determine which content will be delivered interactively, and develop learning activities.

As portions of a project are completed, there are checkpoints at which team members can review and fine-tune the progress. The site evolves through alpha and beta stages before learners are ready to use it. As students are enlisted, evaluation of the site structure and content is valuable for future consideration.

Some barriers to success can be avoided. Issues of language, communication, time and space, and work styles all come into play. Designers may have difficulty resisting the urge to revise until the last possible moment.

Finally, new distance learning developers are learners in the online environment too. Lessons about organization, the structure of Web-based information, and the applicability of Web functionality to familiar content are valuable.

When the curtain comes down on a course's premiere, there's celebrating to do. But after the classroom goes dark, the players have the opportunity to regroup, rethink, and even retool before the next audience arrives.

REFERENCES

Jacob, David. 1997. *Data Transmission Speeds* [Online]. Available: www.xist.com/jakob/speed2.html [19 October 2000].

Schrum, Lynne. 1998. "On-Line Education: A Study of Emerging Pedagogy." In *Adult Learning and the Internet*, edited by Brad Cahoon. San Francisco: Jossey-Bass Publishers.

Wiesenberg, F., and S. Hutton. 1996. "Teaching a Graduate Program Using Computer-Mediated Conferencing Software." *Journal of Distance Education*, 11, no 1: 83–100.

Chapter 5

Renew and Retool: New Skills for the Distance Educator

To some, teaching a course online has a lot of appeal. It can mean working from home in pajamas while drinking hot chocolate. If one is teaching in an asynchronous environment it also means teaching at odd hours and whenever it fits the instructor's schedule. It sounds like a dream come true to many educators.

While everything stated may be true, it doesn't mean that being a successful educator in a distance learning environment is easily accomplished. As mentioned in Chapter 4, teaching in an electronic environment doesn't simply mean that you take the content covered in a face-to-face classroom format and use it on the Web. Instead you need to rethink everything about the course, from core concepts and outcomes to effective methods of course delivery.

When teaching in a live format you probably see students once or twice a week for up to three hours. Then you might see a few more during weekly office hours. When teaching online students will be in contact with you twenty-four hours a day, seven days a week. No matter what time of day you check your e-mail, Sunday through Saturday 12 a.m. to midnight, you'll probably find several messages from the students in your class. (For this reason some who teach in a distance learning environment inform students they will only read and respond to e-mail on certain days of the week.)

Regular contact with students is just one of the ingredients for success in a distance learning classroom. In this chapter you'll find out about others, including presentation and selection of content, handling "problem" students, and motivating students to keep on track and keep online.

STARTING FROM SCRATCH: SELECTING AND PREPARING CONTENT

Keys to online teaching are the course design, how the content is delivered, and how the instructor interacts with students as they progress through the course. However, course development is the most important of these components. Thus there is a clear distinction between teaching online and teaching a traditional course. Although planning is obviously involved in traditional instruction, the planning requirements for developing online instruction are much more stringent. An instructor who is also the developer of the course to be taught online must approach the development with the understanding that what is done in development constitutes the lion's share of the online teaching process. This shift requires a different mindset from that needed for teaching a traditional course (Meyen and Lian, 1997).

Chapter 4 detailed what goes into developing a Web-based distance learning experience and briefly discussed making decisions about course content and course format. In this chapter the focus is more on the specifics of how to take content and put it together for online presentation.

For starters, imagine you are going to teach a course on reference policies, procedures, and services online for the first time. Just last semester you taught the class in a face-to-face format and are familiar with the content. What you need to do now is figure out what content will work well in the online format, what needs to be reformatted, and what you might just have to throw away.

As you get started you think about the student outcomes for the course. At the same time you consider how in the past you ensured those outcomes were met when teaching in the live classroom format. For example, perhaps a student outcome for the course is to make sure students understand the steps in the research process and the library's role in helping customers complete those steps. In the past you achieved that goal by spending a three-hour class period going over the steps in the process with students and brainstorming, with the full class and small groups, about how the library fits into the process. Before coming to class students read a few articles on the topic and after the class is over they are required to work in small groups to develop a research process checklist for libraries.

Now the question becomes, "is that same outcome possible in an online format even though you might not use the same techniques to disseminate the information?" Most likely the answer is "yes." Here's what's different. Instead of meeting for a three-hour period one day during the week, students immerse themselves in the topic for an entire week by taking part in discussion board conversation and they meet with their peers using chat to develop their online research process checklist. In this example the difference between online learning and live classroom experience isn't very large. The biggest difference is that you won't be standing in front of the class facilitating a discussion on the topic. Instead you will be doing the facilitating from the course Web site by leading the online discussions.

Looking at a different example demonstrates how format and content can change when moving from face-to-face presentation to an online one. Now imagine that you are teaching a young-adult literature course online. In the live version of the course you usually cover booktalking techniques. The way you accomplish this is by spending a portion of one class going over good booktalking techniques, having a librarian come to the class to demonstrate how to perform booktalks, and then requiring students to present a series of booktalks to their classmates over the course of the semester. You probably believe that booktalking is an integral part of library services to teens so you don't want to throw away that piece of the course, but you may have trouble figuring out how to give students what they require in the online environment.

In order to solve this problem you need to look closely at the technology available to you and to your students. As discussed in Chapter 4, if your students can't handle applications that require lots of bandwith then it's not worth integrating those applications into your online class. For that reason you might have to decide that streaming video of successful booktalks over the course Web site is a bad idea. However, don't forget there are other forms of technology available. Instead of the streaming video you might create a CD-ROM that all students receive when they register for the course. The CD would include sample booktalks performed by a variety of librarians.

During the week that you cover booktalks, students would be required to view the CD-ROM booktalks and you would facilitate an online discussion on what makes a good booktalk and on different booktalking techniques. Still missing, however, is practice creating and presenting booktalks to peers. This is something that you might need to rethink. If students don't have access to video equipment or video conferencing technologies integrating booktalk presentations into the class might be impossible. Students can certainly create booktalks and post them on the course Web site for critique and review by their classmates. But you just might not be able to go the distance with the presentation piece of the puzzle.

As noted in Chapter 4, and as you can see from the above examples, certain types of content lend themselves more easily to online learning. If you are working with a piece of content that does seem to be impossible to teach online, try to be as creative as possible about what you might do to get the idea across.

Selecting the Format

Of course, as you select the content you are also making decisions about how it will be presented to students. You need to decide which topics lend themselves to large group discussions, which will work best in small group discussions, and which will work best via chat. Then think about when you might want to add interactive components in which students take part in an online learning activity in order to understand the concept being presented.

Examples of what's appropriate for different formats include the following:

- Discussions regarding broad topics and concepts work well in the discussion board format. In this model the instructor posts a topic for discussion and then students respond to the instructor's posting and to comments from their peers. This format provides students with the chance to think about their response before posting. Some students might actually take 24 hours or more to consider the ideas expressed and compose their response. This format is ideal for book discussions in literature classes and when covering broad issues of policies, procedures, and customer services.
- Topics that have lots of subtlety work well as part of small group chat sessions. In these discussions students converse just like they do in a classroom, focusing on complex and abstract concepts in real time. Chat is ideal for discussions on intellectual freedom and copyright issues and when guest speakers are invited to participate in the class.
- Learning activities work well for content in which students learn best by doing. These include lessons where students are required to seek out particular pieces of information or when they need to learn how to use a new tool or resource. Online learning activities work well in information literacy classes in which students practice using research tools and then answer a series of questions about those tools to evaluate and cement their learning.

Preparing the Content

Once you decide what you are going to include in your online course, and the format in which it will be presented, you need to prepare the materials for students. The preparation includes developing the online components, as discussed in Chapter 4, and developing print or electronic resources that will be used to complement the online materials. At the University of Maine at Augusta Library and Information Technology Distance Education Program, instructors develop course manuals. These manuals are distributed via postal mail to students when they register for a course.

The paper manual provides students with a step-by-step outline of what will be covered in the course, what the instructor's expectations are, what will be covered week to week, and how to deal with any technical glitches that might arise. In other words it's an extended syllabus. Jana Bradley at Syracuse University noted that one of the biggest differences between live and online teaching was in this type of preparation. She said, "The differences are, for me, using online components requires much more advance preparation, preferably before the semester starts. Much more has to be written down; structuring discussion needs to be done in advance; online formats encourage preparation of lists of websites [sic] or online resources" (2000).

At this point you might be asking yourself, why do students need paper if everything is online? It's a good question. Students can carry their manual around with them and look things up when they need to. They can keep track of course requirements without having to go online. In other words it gives students a sense of security, particu-

---

Figure 5–1: Sample Page from Course Manual: What About Reference Space/Assignment?

Week 7–What About the Reference Space—March 5 – March 11

- Read pages 111 to 121 in the textbook.

- Visit a library and walk around the reference area and answer the observation questions about space that are posted on the class web site. (If you have been to the library before try to look around as if you have never been in the facility before.)

- After you have answered the questions interview a reference librarian at the same library about what he/she thinks are the strengths and weaknesses of the space (sample questions on the class web site).

- Visit the discussion board and post your findings from the observation what you learned from the librarian about the space.

Pathfinder Due

---

larly students who aren't completely comfortable with technology.

Figure 5–1 shows a section of a course manual where you see how the week's tasks are outlined for students. Students know they have to participate in online discussion, they know they have to read part of the textbook, they know they have to use the observation protocols on the course Web site, and they know they have to interview a reference librarian. Since the instructor isn't in front of students informing them of what they need to do and when, the course manual provides the kind of information that is required in order for a student to be successful in the class.

CONSIDERING THE STUDENT

Student success is of course the most important aspect of what needs to be achieved via an online class. It can't be assumed that if the course content is good and the Web presentation is good, that students will automatically have a successful learning experience. Online and face-to-face teaching both require that teachers find methods for interacting with and leading students through the content in order to achieve learning.

In March 2000 the National Education Association (NEA) and courseware provider, Blackboard, Inc., published a list of benchmarks for distance education. In the category of "Teaching and Learning," two of the benchmarks are:

- Student interaction with faculty and other students is an essential characteristic and is facilitated through a variety of ways, including voice-mail and/or e-mail.
- Feedback to student assignments and questions is constructive and provided in a timely manner (National Education Association and Blackboard, Inc., 2000).

While learning online builds a community between students and instructors it can also be an isolating experience. As a result, students require that their online teachers communicate with them regularly about course content and course assignments. If that communication doesn't take place students tend to feel they are drifting on their own without an anchor. When asked what she liked least about teaching online, Cheryl McCarthy from the University of Rhode Island said, "The expectation that the instructor is available 24–7 online and the anxiety of responding ASAP to questions posted, etc." (2000).

Imagine what students in a distance learning class might look like when they "attend" the class. It's possible that they are sitting in front of a computer in a room in their house. Most likely they are the only person in the room at the moment. However, outside the door there might be kids who are doing their own homework, a husband or wife who just got home from work, or roommates planning what they are going to be doing that night. While they are logged onto the course Web site, they spend time looking at the materials available for the week and take part in asynchronous discussions with their classmates. Although they are in a house with other people just outside the door, and although they are participating in class, they never speak a word aloud for the hour or two in which they are in class on this particular day.

COMMUNICATING PROFESSIONALLY

Just as you develop methods and strategies for presenting the course content electronically, you also need to develop methods and strategies for interacting with students in an online class in order to make sure they understand the content and to make sure that their sense of isolation is lessened. Some questions that arise from educators in the online environment include:

- Do I have to respond to every e-mail from every student in a class?

- Is it necessary to respond to every posting on the class discussion board?
- How does one handle students who communicate inappropriately when using communication features of the class Web site?
- What does one do about poor grammar and spelling in electronic discussion?
- How does one make sure that students understand the assignments as outlined in the course syllabus?

Each of these is an important question and bears careful consideration. In answering each one it's a good idea to balance student needs with instructional goals. One of the most important things an instructor, in any venue, can do is to let students know what's acceptable and expected on the first day of class. In the online environment that might mean that on the first official day of class the instructor posts an announcement on the course Web site outlining specific expectations about performance and communication.

Perhaps expectations are covered in a course manual that is distributed to students before the first day of class. As a part of these expectations the instructor might set guidelines for sending and responding to e-mail, he or she might specify what type of discussion board postings he or she will respond to; the instructor can provide rules for appropriate communication and a sample of a well-written discussion board posting and chat communication.

It's possible, even probable, that even though the instructor is clear about expectations from the beginning, some students will not understand them fully. That means they will have to be handled on a case-by-case basis during the timeframe for the class.

Responding to E-Mail

Students find e-mail an easy and effective way to communicate with instructors. It is one of the technologies with which they are comfortable. As mentioned earlier in this chapter, that could mean that as an instructor you will receive many e-mails every day and at all hours of the day. Many students will send written assignments as attachments and will want to know that you have received their work successfully. These tips on setting up e-mail communication to meet both student and instructor needs should prove helpful:

- When the course begins inform students of how long they should expect to wait for a response to an e-mail message. Tell them if you will respond within eight hours, twelve hours, twenty-four hours, seventy-two hours, or some other timeframe.
- At the outset of the course set up guidelines for the type of e-mail you expect to receive and how you will respond. For example, inform students that sending written assignments via e-mail is acceptable and that you will send a message saying the assignment has been received. Let students know they can send you e-mail about course delivery and content and that you will respond within the timeframe you set up for responses. Also let students know that e-mails that do not ask a specific question or that do not demand an answer may not merit a response.

- As the class begins inform students if sending draft versions of written assignments via e-mail is acceptable. The nature of e-mail makes this a very alluring proposition for students. However, if the instructor is not able to spend the time necessary to read and comment on the drafts, students should know ahead of time that this is not acceptable.
- As soon as you receive an e-mail message with an assignment attached inform the student that receipt was successful. In the same message you can let the student know when they should expect to receive feedback on the assignment. However, don't provide a timeframe unless you are certain that you can meet the deadlines you set.

Discussion Board Facilitation

Many instructors in distance education programs find that discussion boards are a successful means of emulating live class discussions. Depending on the makeup of an online class and the topic up for discussion, these boards often end up being lively forums for debate. When this happens, an instructor might find an overwhelming number of postings to read and respond to on a daily basis. Similarly, the number of postings they need to read and respond to may overwhelm students. Consider these options when figuring out how to handle discussion board postings:

- At the outset of the class set some guidelines for what is expected of students regarding reading and responding to discussion board postings. Some instructors set a timeframe for initial postings on the discussion board. For example, if there are weekly discussions that begin on Monday, an instructor might tell students they need to post at least one message to the board by Friday of each week. This helps students manage their time and ensures that at the end of the discussion board period there are not a lot of late postings that require reading and to which he or she needs to respond.

- During early class discussions the instructor should be as active as possible, responding to most, if not all, postings in order to help students feel comfortable with the format, the class, and each other. As the class moves forward the instructor may be more selective in his or her responses to the postings, replying specifically to those postings that make an important point or which warrant careful consideration and response.

- Let students know if they are expected to read every posting on the discussion board. Some instructors inform students that they are only required to read postings originated by the instructor and in response to the instructor's postings. Other instructors specify the exact number of postings a student must read. Think carefully about this decision. If students are not required to read every posting, it's important to find other means to make sure that students are getting the full content of the discussion.

- Remember that students may feel isolated as they are doing their coursework. As that is sometimes the case, make sure to be an equal opportunity responder. Even though some students in the class will always have interesting things to say, others will not—make sure to respond to everyone equally so no student thinks he or she is being left out of the discussion.

- As students become familiar with the discussion board and are more comfortable with each other, use the board to stimulate conversation among students. Post provocative questions on a particular topic and let students "talk" to each other about the topic without the interference of the instructor.

Inappropriate Communication

Inappropriate communication in a distance learning environment can take on a variety of forms. These might include inappropriate responses to online or e-mail discussions and bombarding the instructor with e-mails that do not relate specifically to the content of the course. Because students in online classes feel not only isolated but also anonymous, they may believe they can communicate in ways that would not be acceptable in a live classroom. Also, some students do not realize the differences inherent in online and live communication. That means they require specific guidelines on how to communicate successfully in an online environment. The following scenarios and solutions provide ideas on how to handle inappropriate communication:

- Some students in the class see themselves as experts on the topic under discussion. When they communicate with other students, they assert their ideas strongly and, by referring to other students by name in their communications, they create the impression that they are confronting those students and their ideas. As the instructor, you notice this and you see that student communication in the class is dwindling rapidly. To rectify the situation you take a two-pronged approach. First, you post an announcement on the course Web site stating guidelines for communication on the course Web site and presenting ideas on what makes online communication different than face-to-face communication. Second, you contact the students who are communicating inappropriately—either by e-mail or phone—and go over the information presented on the Web site directly with them. This solution accomplishes two things. First, by posting the announcement, you let students know that you are aware of the situation and you are taking care of it. Second, by directly contacting the students in question, you can be sure they know that you consider their communication technique inappropriate and that you are willing to help them find better ways to get their points across.

- One of the students in the class is sending you e-mail complaints about the format of the class, the grades he or she receives, and the sponsoring institution. He or she also put you on his or her jokes distribution list so that you receive several e-mails daily of jokes that he or she thinks will amuse friends and instructors. Handle the situation directly. As soon as you realize what is happening, contact the student via phone or e-mail. When you communicate with him or her, you need to state clearly what types of e-mail messages are acceptable and what are not. At the same time it's important to give the student options for having his or her comments and issues addressed. Let the student know that if he or she has questions about the course delivery or content he or she should summarize them in one e-mail and send that to you. Inform the student of how they can make their concerns about the sponsoring institution heard by contacting the appropriate staff members. Also, inform him or her of what types of e-mail messages you will respond to and what types you won't. Make sure the student knows you are open to appropriate feedback and that you are willing to respond to questions that will help him or her succeed in the class.

Writing Style Concerns

Gale Eaton from the University of Rhode Island noted that distance education is not a good learning format for students who can't write. Expressing thoughts in a written format is an important component of online teaching. Since students are not meeting with the instructor and classmates face-to-face, they need to communicate primarily through the written word. As a result it's important for students to know what is expected in their writing when communicating electronically with classmates or the instructor. It's useful for the instructor to set up guidelines related to these expectations and make sure students are able to follow them (Eaton, 2000). The following tips are useful when determining how to deal with writing style concerns in online instruction:

- Include on the class Web site, in the course manual, or both, a style sheet for electronic communication.

This should include tips for how to compose a successful e-mail message and discussion board posting. If possible include examples of good and bad messages in each format.

- Provide students with guidance regarding the differences between communications types. For example, if you are going to be using chat with students let them know that because of the immediacy of that form of communication spelling and grammar will be less important than simply getting ideas out to those also taking part in the chat.

- When you encounter a student who is unable to get his or her ideas across clearly in writing, communicate with them immediately. Make sure the student knows the importance of writing clearly in the electronic format and if they need writing assistance, provide them with information on how to get that help.

Understanding Assignments

Consider this: An instructor in an online course puts together the syllabus and course manual very carefully. The instructor is certain that all the requirements for the course are clearly stated and that assignments are well defined. He or she told students if they had any questions about the assignments they should let him or her know. The time comes for students to "hand-in" their first assignment. As the instructor starts reading the submissions he or she realizes no one understood the assignment at all.

At this point the instructor would certainly realize that something had gone wrong. One of the questions to ask is how to ensure that the same thing doesn't happen again.

The next time the instructor teaches the class he or she might:

- Provide students with a place on the course Web site to communicate about course assignments. For example, the instructor could create a discussion board specifically for this purpose. Students would go there to post their questions, read other students' questions, and read instructor responses. Most likely if one student has a question on an assignment others have the exact same question. In a face-to-face classroom, instructors often ask students if they have questions about assignments. The only way to re-create that type of conversation online is through a discussion board or other form of electronic communication.
- Provide samples of the type of work expected for each assignment. This is something that instructors often do in a live class. In an online environment it becomes even more important as students do not have the same opportunities to get feedback from the instructor on expectations. The samples might be provided on the course Web site, in the course manual, or in another format.

CONCLUSION

If you consider the concepts noted above regarding preparation and selection of course content and student communication and motivation you will realize that what is required is common sense, practice, and planning. No matter what format you are teaching in you need to find ways to help students succeed. In online teaching this means using electronic media to the best of your capabilities and making sure students can use the same to the best of their capabilities. This includes determining what content works well in an online environment and finding the best means to make sure students have what they need in order to be successful.

When asked what she liked about teaching in an online environment Gale Eaton at the University of Rhode Island stated, "I like the student-centeredness. Students have been cooperative and mutually supportive in the class discussions, and they have offered some very thoughtful and informative material to their classmates. I'm sure it's taking them more time, also, but the quality of participation seems higher than in the traditional classroom" (2000).

Preparing to teach and keeping students motivated and on task in the distance learning environment requires a big investment of your time. However, as Gale's comments demonstrate, taking the time necessary bears important rewards for you and your students.

REFERENCES

Bradley, Jana. 2000. Telephone interview with Linda Braun, Syracuse, N.Y., December 18.

Eaton, Gale. 2000. Telephone interview with Linda Braun, Kingston, R.I., October 20.

McCarthy, Cheryl. 2000. Telephone interview with Linda Braun, Kingston, R.I., November 27.

Meyen, Edward L., and Cindy H.T. Lian. 1997. "Teaching Online Courses." *Focus on Autism and Other Developmental Disabilities*, 12, no. 3: 166–75.

National Education Association and Blackboard, Inc. 2000. NEA and Blackboard Inc. *Study Finds 24 Measures of Quality in Internet-Based Distance Learning* [Online]. Available: www.ihep.com/PR17.html [22 November 2000].

Chapter 6

Handle with Care: Assessment of Distance Education Students' Needs

"We have found that success in an online course depends as much on one's motivation and surrounding environment for learning as it does on technical capacity." That's from the "Disposition Readiness" section of the Lesley University Graduate School of Education, "Technology in Education Readiness Survey for Participation in Online Courses" (Lesley University, 2000). The statement points out some of the key ingredients related to student success for taking distance learning courses. Students who enroll in a distance learning experience need more than a specific level of academic achievement. They also need to embrace a set of academic and technological competencies in order to succeed in the distance education environment. Therefore, two questions that need consideration are:

- How do students know if they have the requisite academic and technological skills to succeed and how do content providers know they are ready?

- Once enrolled in a distance learning program, what do students require in order to achieve success?

We answer these two questions in this chapter. If you work in a library and are wondering what it would take in order to be a successful student in a distance learning environment, you'll find some answers here. As you read through the chapter think about the requirements we outline and ask yourself, "does this sound like me?"

Or, if you work in a library and would like to provide support to distance learners who use your resources, the information in this chapter will better help you understand what distance learning requires from students. As you read through the chapter consider the distance learners who come into your library. Do you have ideas on how you might help them meet the requirements of distance learners outlined here?

STUDENT READINESS

The Lesley University Web site is just one of the many that post a survey to help students assess their distance learning readiness. Most of these surveys divide the assessment into at least two categories: academic readiness and technological readiness. Let's start by looking at the academic readiness category.

Academic Readiness

On its distance learners self-assessment Web page, Tallahassee Community College notes that distance learners succeed because they are highly motivated, independent, and
active learners with good organizational skills, good time
management skills, and discipline. The students will study
and work without external reminders and are adaptive and
open to new learning environments (Tallahassee Community College, 2000). To determine if a student has these
characteristics, a student pre-assessment must focus on several different categories of academic readiness. These include:

- The ability to work independently. Students enrolled
  in distance learning courses do not have the chance
  to ask instructors or classmates for immediate feedback on course content or assignments. Students must
  be self-directed and feel comfortable working through
  problems independently. They must also be able to
  cope with delayed gratification, waiting, perhaps up
  to a week, for an answer to a question.
- The ability to problem solve. Because students enrolled
  in distance learning courses usually do not have the
  opportunity for instantaneous feedback, they often
  need to figure out answers and solutions on their own.
  This means everything from determining where to locate required reading to finding the e-mail address of
  a fellow student. Problem solving takes creativity and
  flexibility.
- The ability to speak up. Students enrolled in distance
  learning courses need to be willing and able to contact the instructor via e-mail, phone, or alternative

means to ask for information or clarification that they require. In the distance learning environment students don't always have the luxury of hearing the questions and answers of other students. For this reason it's important that a distance learner be able to speak up for himself or herself in order to get the information he or she needs. This active engagement is noted in a section of the PBS Adult Learning Service Web site, "Students who do well in distance learning courses are usually comfortable contacting the instructor as soon as they need help with the course" (PBS Adult Learning Service, 2000).

- The ability to plan ahead. The unavailability of instantaneous feedback also means that a student needs to take an early look at course requirements. He or she will have to explore and determine whether there are questions that require answers or if he or she will need access to specific resources that aren't available locally. If a distance education student waits until the week an assignment is due to ask questions or get resources, he or she might find that it's just too late to access the required information.

- The ability to keep to a schedule and be disciplined. Many students enrolled in distance learning courses do not need to attend class at a particular time on a particular day. Instead it's up to the student to set his or her own timetable and make sure he or she keeps up with the course work according to the required schedule. When taking a distance education course the student needs to be able to turn off the TV and say no to social invitations from family and friends. Of course, the same might be true for students enrolled

Figure 6–1: Tallahassee Community College e-Campus Self-Assessment.

Are you a good candidate for a distance learning course?

Please consider the following self-assessment survey. Think about each question and answer it honestly. YOU have the most to win or lose by taking this survey.

1. What is your reason for taking this class?
   a. I NEED it for a degree, job promotion, or other very important reason.
   b. I thought it might be a nice change, although I could take the class on-campus.
   c. I just wanted to.

2. Do you work well independently?
   a. Yes, I rarely need to be reminded to get a job done.
   b. Sometimes, I can use an occasional reminder or I let things slip by.
   c. Not really, I need someone to keep me on-target - like in a structured classroom.

3. How do you classify your study habits?
   a. I often get things done ahead of time and I even do extra work in order to study the material.
   b. I need reminders and reinforcement to get my studying done.
   c. I do most things at the last minute.

4. Do you like the idea of learning "on your own" with the instructor as a facilitator?
   a. I like it - I enjoy learning on my own and often find that reading the textbook gives me enough insight into the material.
   b. I think I can do it - however, I do like having the instructor lecture on the material after I have read it.
   c. I'm not sure I can learn the material without the instructor telling me what to focus on and without having a lecture as clarification.

5. Often, distance learning courses involve a great deal of reading. Think about your reading skills. How would you classify your reading ability?
   a. Good - I understand articles/textbooks without help.
   b. OK - but I sometimes miss the main point of the material.
   c. Slower than average - I usually need someone to explain textbook material.

6. How are my time management skills?
   a. I am a GREAT manager of time - I create schedules and I stick to them.
   b. I am pretty good - I usually get things done on time.
   c. I'll answer this later!

in traditional classes. However, since there are no specific class meeting dates in most distance learning models, students may feel they can procrastinate more than is actually feasible or viable. Margaret Morrisey, a student in the Central Massachusetts Regional Library System's Basic Library Techniques on Administration course, summed this up when she spoke about what it takes to be a good student in a remote learning environment. It requires, she said, "Discipline

Figure 6–2: Oregon Network for Education/Self-Assessment for Distance Learning.

Self-Assessment for Distance Learning

OREGON NETWORK for EDUCATION

Home | Info Desk | Courses | Degrees | Services | Career Info

Take this quiz to see if you would be a good distance learner

Are you ready to take a distance education course or participate in a distance learning program? Find out by taking the Distance Learning Readiness Self-Assessment. Read each statement and decide if the statement best describes you in four different areas: learning environment; life and academic skills; course expectations; and technology. Keep track of the total number of "yes" answers, and use this number to determine your readiness for distance learning.

		Your Learning Environment
Y	N	I have a specific place where I will be able to study and work on my course assignments.
Y	N	The place I will study is relatively free from interruptions.
		Your Life and Academic Skills
Y	N	I am a self-motivated student.
Y	N	I complete what I start.
Y	N	I am able to work independently with little direction.
Y	N	I am capable of self-discipline.
Y	N	I am an organized person who is able to structure my own time and surroundings.
Y	N	I do not get easily discouraged when I run into difficulties.
Y	N	I believe that what I learn or do not learn is ultimately my own responsibility.
Y	N	I think of myself as a good student (e.g., take good notes, prepare and study for examinations, write well, employ good study habits).
Y	N	I am capable of doing college-level work.
Y	N	I can read for comprehension from a range of materials: books, journals, websites, etc.

with one's time and good organizational ability" (2000).

- The ability to read and comprehend class materials. Students enrolled in distance learning courses do need to have the appropriate reading and language skills required of students enrolled in more traditional learning experiences. That means they must be able to read and understand the course materials without the benefit of contextual exchanges.

Now we've taken a look at the characteristics required of a distance learning student. The question then becomes: "How does a student know these characteristics are required and how do education providers know that students are aware of these requirements?" This is where student readiness pre-assessments come in. Educational institutions from around the country have created everything from checklists to online forms to make sure that students understand what is required of them academically. Figures 6–1 and 6–2 show the types of questions and formats provided by academic institutions.

You will notice the questions asked on each of these surveys directly relate to the characteristics listed above. The key then is to make sure that students answer the survey honestly and that the sponsoring institution aids the student in making a good decision about the type of education offerings in which he or she should enroll.

Though the virtual classroom is a great opportunity for many, some people simply lack the characteristics that make good distance learners. To avoid frustrated and disaffected learners, it's best for everyone to recognize that in advance. For those who are strong distance learning candidates, technological readiness is the next prerequisite.

Technological Readiness

Before a student enrolls in a distance education course that is based primarily online, it's important that he or she be familiar with the technology required in order to succeed.

Students need to understand the minimum hardware and software requirements of the course and what's available to them locally. Included in the technology specification checklist should be:

- Operating system
- Processor
- Memory
- Hard drive space
- A/V, including audio and video playback
- Software, including Web browser (and the version), e-mail package, word processing, and any other specific applications required by the course
- Level of Internet access (high speed, modem, etc.)
- Approximate time required (daily and weekly) for Internet access

Owning, or access to, the technology is only the first step however. Once students are sure they have the technology required, they also need to make sure they know how to use it. Institutions that provide distance learning opportunities handle this in a couple of different ways.

- Some institutions make technical competencies a part of the residential orientation they require before students begin their first class. In these instances students have in-class instruction on each of the components necessary and the opportunity to practice.
- Other institutions inform students of the requirements and then assume they will be fulfilled. Difficulties then might arise if the student lacks the knowledge to un-

Figure 6–3: Checklist for Student Distance Learning Success.			
	Yes	No	N/A
I have the technology required to participate.			
I received all course materials sent out by the sponsoring institution.			
I read the course materials.			
I know how to contact the instructor.			
I know how to access the course Web site.			
I know how to use the course Web site successfully.			
I know how to access any materials required in order to complete the course—articles, books, etc.			
I know how to contact classmates if I need to.			
I know how to receive technical support if need be.			
I made a schedule of tasks, with due dates, that need to be completed in order to successfully finish the course.			
This is the information I need to find out from the instructor or the sponsoring institution before the class is completed. (Include the dates by which the information must be located.)			

derstand the technological terms and assumes he or she will figure them out along the way.

- Another approach is to provide students with access to online tutorials that might help them in gaining the

Figure 6–4: Student Weekly Checklist.

Week 1   January 7–21

❑ Chapters 1 & 2
❑ Discussion Board Introduction
❑ Discussion Board—Reference Service Definition
❑ Discussion Board—Response

Week 2   January 22–28

❑ Chapter 3 & pp 175–181
❑ Learning Style Inventory
❑ Discussion Board—Learning Styles List
❑ Discussion Board—Response
❑ Web Site Update (Friday!)

Week 3   January 29–February 4

❑ Article 1
❑ Article 2
❑ Article 3
❑ Discussion Board—Information Literacy/Research Process
❑ Discussion Board—Response
❑ Web Site Update

Week 4   February 5–11

❑ Appendix A
❑ Interview Librarian
❑ Discussion Board—Reference Policies
❑ Discussion Board—Reference Scenario
❑ Discussion Board—Response
❑ Web Site Update

Chart created and designed by Ann Kampersal, University of Maine at Augusta, Library and Information Technology program, Winter 2001.

technical competencies they require. For students to access the online tutorials, they need at least a limited amount of prior technical knowledge. Assuming the students' prior knowledge is not necessarily a reliable practice on the part of the teaching organization.

- There are also institutions that send students a list of print and online resources that will help them gain the required technical competencies. This approach also assumes ability on the part of the student.

No matter which tack an institution takes, when students begin their first courses, some will no doubt require technical and academic assistance.

ONCE THE PROGRAM BEGINS

When a student enrolls in a distance learning course it can prove useful for him or her to use a checklist or some other form of graphical organizer to make sure he or she is on the right track before the first day of class. Figure 6–3 is an example of the type of device that might be used by students. Figure 6–4 is an example of how a student can make sure he or she continues to stay on track throughout the duration of the class.

Beyond staying on track and organized, students also need to find and maintain a support structure. Support will help them through what can be an isolating experience. When asked if the distance learning experience met her expectations, Margaret Morrisey replied, "During the course I experienced many frustrations due to my inexperience and lack of understanding of the technology and its performance. However, I learned as I went along. Another colleague and I tended to stay in touch with regard to our progress and we even met a couple of times. This relationship seemed to greatly improve our progress vis a vis the other students" (2000).

Students enrolled in distance learning courses often report that they find ways to "meet" with their classmates on a regular basis. They report e-mailing each other to talk about course content and instruction. In this way students provide one another with a support group very much like meeting in a student union or the halls of an institution. This kind of peer support is essential in helping to ensure that a learning experience is successful. In order for students to attain this support structure they must of course have easy access to the e-mail addresses of their classmates, and that's the responsibility of the instructor or the sponsoring institution.

Handling the Technology

One of the biggest frustrations students encounter is technology. As mentioned above, even if they have the necessary hardware and software and technical competencies problems can occur. As a result, students need to feel comfortable and confident in contacting the appropriate technical support and in finding a speedy resolution to the difficulty. As noted in Chapter 3, startup distance learning programs often suffer technical difficulties of their own. It's important that students aren't left feeling that they are responsible for those problems and understand that a resolution is sought.

In her article, "Coping in a Distance Environment: Sitcoms, Chocolate Cake, and Dinner with a Friend," Michelle M. Kazmer sums up the need for students to feel confident and comfortable with technical support this way, "When students have difficulties using their computers, software, or communications systems, they find the problems more readily solved if there are familiar individuals who can provide timely and reliable technology support. Students describe these people as consistent, available, and extremely patient. Students also say that these characteristics make them more comfortable in using the technology and testing its limits, in turn making them more skilled in its use" (Kazmer, 2000).

It's possible to see how students can gain the requisite comfort and confidence by looking at the Central Massachusetts Regional Library System's Basic Library Techniques online class. When the region offered the course, the system's technical specialist wore a pager twenty-four hours a day, seven days a week. During the program's face-to-face orientation session, he informed students that he would be available to help them with their technical difficulties at any time day or night. Although they did not contact him in the middle of the night, students enrolled in the course appreciated the commitment. It gave many of them the confidence and comfort they needed in order to contact the technical specialist when there was a problem. The evaluation of the program highlights this point, "Access to quick and efficient technical support [was a success]. Students noted how important it was to be able to contact someone to ask questions about the course and their use of the Web site. Students unanimously agreed that the technical support they received in order to make use of the site was excellent. They praised Rick Levine for his availability and patience in helping students figure out how to access the various components of the course" (Braun, 2000:4).

Knowing Who to Call

It's not only important for students to know who and how to contact technical support. It's also important that they know whom to contact for other types of information at the sponsoring institution. For example, they need easy access to information about financial aid, grades, course registration, and other administrative details. This type of contact information should be included in the course Web site and the course manual. Since it's part of the support system that helps to make students feel secure, all of the supporting information should be provided online and in hard copy.

CONCLUSION

In a distance learning environment, students are responsible for their success in different ways than in a traditional classroom environment. Distance learning students often need to take the first step in order to locate information, get answers to questions, and find out how to fix a technical or academic problem. They don't have the "luxury" of being surrounded by classmates who might be willing to help them solve problems. Instead they need to rely on their own abilities and problem-solving techniques.

The institution offering a distance learning course and

the instructor teaching the course can help students along the way. But it is ultimately up to the student to display the requisite characteristics and be proactive in his or her learning in order to succeed. As Margaret Morrissey stated when asked what made someone a good candidate for distance learning, "Being prepared to try new things. Being unafraid or unabashed to ask for assistance and clarification is a big help" (2000).

REFERENCES

Braun, Linda W. 2000. *Massachusetts Online Distance Education For Library Staff: MODELS Evaluation of Online Electronic Components*, June.

Kazmer, Michelle M. 2000. *Coping in a Distance Environment: Sitcoms, Chocolate Cake, and Dinner with a Friend*. First Monday, volume 5, number 9 [Online]. Available: www.firstmonday.dk/issues/issue5_9/kazmer/#k3 [4 January 2001].

Lesley University. 2000. *Readiness Survey – Disposition Readiness* [Online]. Available: www.lesley.edu/online_learning/readiness/dispo.html. [4 January 2001].

Morrisey, Margaret. 2000. Telephone interview with Carolyn Noah, Southbridge, Mass., November 21.

PBS Adult Learning Service. 2000. *Locate Courses and Distance Degree Opportunities* [Online]. Available: www.pbs.org/cgi-bin/collegequiz.sh [4 January 2001].

Tallahassee Community College. 2000. *Distance Learning, Self-Assessment* [Online]. Available: www.tcc.cc.fl.us/courses/selfassess.asp. [4 January 2001].

Chapter 7

Look Ahead:
The Future of the
Browsable Classroom

Whether you've devoured *The Browsable Classroom* with relish or approached it with trepidation, it's worthwhile to take a quick look at the some of the major conclusions and directions we've suggested.

THE FACTS OF DISTANCE LEARNING

Distance learning is delivered synchronously or asynchronously, and each approach has benefits and deficits.

Synchronous learning, when students and instructor are assembled at the same time in different places, is presented using live compressed video (for example, Picture Tel) technology or over the Web. Web-based presentations might employ chat or conferencing software. Synchronicity requires that everyone be awake at the same time, posing hurdles for students who are geographically distributed. It also provides immediate gratification and communication, a benefit for many.

Asynchronous learning takes place when the learning community is not assembled at one time. Instructors and students communicate through discussion lists, e-mail, or discussion boards. Learners who can tolerate delayed gratification may find the demands of asynchronous learning to be more palatable than those of synchronous learning.

Many effective programs, either in real time or asynchronous, also provide opportunities for students to meet face-to-face for orientation, discussion, and to build a social network.

Course Web sites provide a focus for work done in the virtual classroom. Web-based courses may use a pre-packaged environment, software referred to as courseware, or they may be developed independently, which often provides both instructors and learners with more flexibility for teaching and learning. In either instance, Web-based courses often incorporate discussion boards and chat as the primary mode of communication between instructors and students and student to student.

EXPANDING OPTIONS FOR DISTANCE LEARNERS

A wide range of courses is available for learners from youth through adulthood. They range from online tutorials, full-length courses, and informal interactive learning experiences. Courses can be self-studies or instructor led. An effective marriage between text and interactivity makes online learning engaging and personal.

As varied as the range of courses available are the types of providers of distance learning. Some are commercial providers, others non-profit educational sources. The American Library Association offers a growing range of continuing education for librarians through its divisions as well as some learning opportunities for families. Academic and public libraries offer content, for staff and customers, ranging from computer skills to research strategies. The Association of College & Research Libraries (ACRL) has codified the elements of good Web-based learning with its "Tips for Developing Effective Web-Based Library Instruction" (ACRL, Instruction Section Methods Committee, 2000). The guidelines confirm that interactivity is an important element for engaging learners successfully.

Though the primary characteristics of current Web-based offerings are diversity in style, structure, and delivery, current collaborative efforts among institutions of higher education and others suggest that options for students will become broader and better as time goes on.

LIBRARIES GET INVOLVED

Though academic libraries have led the way in planning services to support distance learners, public and school libraries have begun to focus on the needs of this new constituency.

Traditional services, especially interlibrary loan and delivery, become even more important when a student is remote from the library or the institution hosting his or her online course. Reference is as important as ever, but may be delivered through e-mail or chat, during regular library hours or in the middle of night.

In addition to traditional library services, some new services are evolving as well. Web-based pathfinders and research guides, proctoring, and hosting equipment for the virtual classroom all place new demands on library staff. Librarians who collaborate with distance instructors find themselves preparing learning resources for students they never see.

Collaboration is key to success in the new environment—whether it's to ensure that learners have access to the materials they need or to train faculty on the complexity of copyright issues that apply to mounting material on the Web.

BUILDING THE ONLINE LIBRARY

Lots of behind-the-scenes work goes into building a distance learning offering. It's complex, unexpectedly demanding of the provider's time, and requires plenty of organizational resources. As a result, the best approach for a first time out is to plan ahead, involve people at all levels of the hosting organization, and stay flexible.

Even when pre-packaged software is used, at least three types of expertise must go into planning a Web-based course. They are technical, educational, and content knowledge. The content specialist is familiar with the subject at hand and sets the learning objectives to be met. The educational specialist oversees instructional design and ensures that the learning opportunities engage learners of all types. The technical team member builds the Web site and programs the interactivity. Alternatively, if courseware is used, he or she makes sure the software is programmed appropriately to ensure successful teaching and learning. All three work in close collaboration for the best results.

Despite best intentions, there are often barriers to success. Among them are issues of language, work styles, and communication. With care, problems can be resolved as the team's work moves onward.

TEACHING IN THE VIRTUAL CLASSROOM

Even the instructor who is a master in his or her field will be required to rethink everything about a course before it goes online, from core concepts and outcomes to effective methods of course delivery. It becomes important to explore the instructional options available through Web technology and carefully match learning objectives to the delivery style most appropriate to them.

For thoughtful and subtle discussion, a real-time environment such as chat may work best. Discussions that are likely to be expansive and broad work on discussion boards, and learning that requires active hands-on engagement may be best encouraged by interactive lessons.

Effective online instructors consider the individual student and provide course handbooks with basic information about using the Web site or courseware and about the institution. Regular and thorough feedback and personal interaction are critically important to prevent the remote learning experience from being isolating. Since students may be in touch at any hour of the day or night, providing feedback can become demanding. It's just as important to be prepared to intervene if students are contributing inappropriately. Common sense, practice, and planning are all required of a successful online instructor.

GOOD CANDIDATES FOR DISTANCE LEARNING

Distance learning isn't for everyone. In fact, some people aren't cut out for it at all. Among important characteristics are the abilities to work independently, problem solve, speak up, plan ahead, keep to a schedule, and be disciplined.

Before making the commitment to distance learning, potential students may want to take a self-assessment to determine whether their learning habits will lead to online success. Technological readiness and a good support system are important too.

CONCLUSION

The flexibility and convenience of distance learning will continue to attract increasing numbers of students of all types. As the field expands, hosting institutions and distance instructors become more expert at developing engaging and challenging offerings and at supporting students effectively. School, public, and academic libraries are meeting the challenge of providing for the informational needs of the new distance learning constituency.

Evolving rapidly to take advantage of the increased flexibility and sophistication of Web capabilities, online learning has the potential to meet the needs of diverse learners at many levels. To achieve its potential, distance learning requires the engagement of the entire learning community—instructors, instructional designers, Web developers, librarians, and students. Their collaboration will ensure the robust future of the browsable classroom.

REFERENCE

Association of College & Research Libraries, Instruction Section Methods Committee. 2000. "Tips for Developing Effective Web-Based Library Instruction" [Online]. Available: www.lib.vt.edu/istm/WebTutorials Tips.html [22 January 2001].

Appendix:
Glossary of Useful Distance
Education Terms

Alpha site—A draft Web site. Functionality is in place, but the work is in progress and fairly rough.

Applications—Computer programs.

Asynchronous—When those involved in a distance learning experience do not communicate in real time.

Audio chat—Online discussion, by voice, requiring the installation of a microphone on the local system, a stable connection and a high speed connection to the Internet.

Bandwith—The measure of the speed of data packets traveling across the Internet. Some examples: T1, T3, 56K.

Beta site—A nearly finished Web site. Functionality and content are in place. There are a few wrinkles to work out.

bps—the abbreviation for bits per second, the standard measure of data transmission speed.

Broadband—High speed Internet connections where the information travels through "broader" lines than those used for telephone modem access. Possible broadband connections include cable modems and satellite.

Chat—A synchronous, text-based mode of online communication.

Chat space—An area of a course Web site devoted to real-time discussion using chat.

Cohort—A group of students who begin and proceed through a program together.

Comp—A composite, a look and feel plan for a Web site.

Compressed video—Audiovisual data transmitted over Internet lines. To economize on the amount of data that must be sent, it is condensed before it is shipped and "unpacked" locally. To use compressed video, both the sender and viewer must generally share the same technology.

Connection speed—The relative speed at which packets of information travel across the Internet to reach the user's computer. Connection speed varies with modems, lines, and Internet traffic.

Content document—The script for an entire Web site, including text, activities, and indications of internal and external links.

Courseware—Software used for delivering course content.

Usually includes an interface for discussion boards, assignment postings, chat, grading, and document delivery. Current popular vendors of courseware include Blackboard and WebCT.

Discussion board—An area of a course Web site where students and instructors post and respond to messages. Sometimes referred to as "threaded" discussions. In a threaded discussion the display of messages is by subject (thread) with comments on the subject (thread) displayed within. Also known as a message board or bulletin boards.

Electronic mailing list—A system of distributing e-mail to a group of people, usually using majordomo or listserv.

Functionality—The way pages of a Web site work together including navigation and interactive components.

HTML (Hypertext Markup Language)—A programming language used to create Web pages.

Icon—A small graphic symbol used consistently to denote the type of information it represents. For example, a star may denote high importance.

Instructional designer—A person who is responsible for making sure that online course content supports pedagogical goals.

Interactivity—Components of a Web site in which the learner is encouraged to participate. Online interactive learning experiences may include quizzes, puzzles, games, and visual exercises. The user's input affects the outcome of the activity.

Interface—The Web site on which the course is mounted, including its look, feel, and structure.

ITV—Interactive television, or compressed video.

Linear learning—When students study a particular topic through content accessed in a specific sequence.

Location independent—Online learning that does not require students and instructor to participate from the same location.

Non-linear learning—Accessing information on a particular topic in a random sequence in order to gain an understanding of the content.

Observation protocols—A series of questions or points to consider when investigating a particular topic.

Pathfinder—A bibliographic tool that gives students tips, techniques, and resources to use in researching a specific subject.

PictureTel—Technology that allows students in one location to communicate in real time—visually and orally—with an instructor and/or students in another location. Sometimes known as compressed video.

Plug-ins—Specialized Web applications that are installed locally to enable a computer to use pages that contain specific functionality. Examples include Shockwave and Flash.

Portal—A gateway to information. In distance learning an institution often provides a Web page that acts as a student's gateway to class materials and online resources.

Pre-assessment—A tool, often a checklist, that helps a student determine whether he or she has the necessary skills and knowledge to participate successfully in a course.

Proctor—To monitor the administration of a test.

Project manager—The person in charge of organizing and managing a project. In a distance learning framework this person is often a Web design or instructional technology specialist who subcontracts with other professionals to create the distance learning site and sometimes the content.

Real time—Participating in an experience at the same moment in time.

Remote access—The ability to use electronic resources from a distant location.

Schematic design—A document showing each content area for a Web site.

Site coordinator—The person who is in charge or making sure students have the materials they need when involved in courses in which they either meet as a group in a particular location or make use of specific resources at a particular location.

Synchronous—When those involved in a distance learning experience communicate in real time.

Technical design—A document that specifies all of the hardware and software required to run a site as well as basic design elements, such as font.

Telephony—Internet-based real-time verbal communication, similar to telephone communication but with bandwith limitations.

Template—A structure and/or design for course components generally provided with courseware. Instructors fit their content, interactive lessons, and evaluative methods into the structure.

Tutorial—A portion of a Web site that provides interactive instruction.

Virtual classroom—An online environment that students access to locate and use course materials.

Walk-through—A Web design's structural layout, showing links and feel but devoid of content.

Web designer—A person responsible for developing the look of a Web site.

Bibliography

American Association of School Librarians.1999. *ICONnect* [Online]. Available: www.ala.org/ICONN/index.html [22 January 2001].

American Library Association. 2000. *Directory of ALA Accredited LIS Programs that Provide Distance Education Opportunities* [Online]. Available: www.ala.org/alaorg/oa/disted.html [22 January 2001].

Association of College & Research Libraries, Instruction Section Methods Committee. 2000. *Tips for Developing Effective Web-Based Library Instruction* [Online]. Available: www.lib.vt.edu/istm/ WebTutorialsTips.html [22 January 2001].

Blackboard, Inc. 2000. *Blackboard.com* [Online]. Available: www.blackboard.com/ [13 December 2000].

Board of Regents, University of Wisconsin System, University of Wisconsin Extension. 1999. *Distance Education Clearinghouse Definitions of Distance Education* [Online]. Available: www.uwex.edu/disted/ definition.html [13 December 2000].

Bowling Green State University. 2000. *FALCON: An Interactive Web Tutorial* [Online]. Available: www.bgsu.edu/colleges/library/infosrv/ tutorial/tutor1.html [22 January 2001].

Central Massachusetts Regional Library System. 1999. "Basic Library Techniques: Administration" [Online]. Available: www.libed2go.org [19 November 2000].

Concord Consortium and the Hudson (Mass.) Public Schools. 1998–2000. *Virtual High School* [Online]. Available: http://vhs.concord.org [26 November 2000].

Connecticut State University. 2000. *Online CSU* [Online]. Available: www.OnlineCSU.ctstateu.edu/ [22 January 2001].

eCollege. 2000. *eCollege.com* [Online]. Available: www.ecollege.com/ [22 January 2001].

Element K. 2000. [Online]. Available: www.elementk.com [3 November 2000].

Florida Online High School. 2000. [Online]. Available: http://fhs.net/ FHSWeb.nsf/Home?Open [26 November 2000]

Ithaca College Library. 2001. *ICYOUSee* [Online]. Available: www.ithaca.edu/library/Training/ICYouSee.html [22 January 2001].

Librarian's Index to the Internet. 2000. [Online]. Available: www.lii.org [4 December 2000].

Multnomah County Library. 2000. *Ask Us Online* [Online]. Available: www.multcolib.org/askus/index.html [28 November 2000].

Oregon Network for Education. 2000. *Self-Assessment for Distance Learning* [Online]. Available: www.oregonone.org/DEquiz.htm [4 January 2001].

Oregon State University, Valley Library. 2000. *The Library and Distance Education: Faculty Support* [Online]. Available: www.orst.edu/dept/ library/distance_ed/facsup.htm [28 November 2000].

Southern Connecticut State University. 2000. *Online Learning Support* [Online]. Available: www.SouthernCT.edu/~brownm/ [22 January 2001].

University at Albany Libraries. 2001. *Internet Tutorials* [Online]. Available: http://library.albany.edu/internet/ [22 January 2001].

WebCT. 2001. WebCT.com [Online]. Available: www.webct.com. [13 December 2000].

Young Adult Library Services Association. 2000. *Working with Teens and Loving It* [Online]. Available: http://members.ala.org/yalsa/edge/ [22 January 2001].

Notes and Credits

Blackboard screen shot reprinted with permission of Blackboard, Inc.

Falcon Tutorial screen shot reprinted with permission of Bowling Green State University.

LEEP, http://leep.lis.uiuc.edu, screen shot reprinted with permission. © Board of Trustees University of Illinois.

Oregon Network for Education *Self-Assessment for Distance Learning* reprinted with permission of the Oregon Network for Education, OregonONE.org.

Student weekly checklist reprinted with permission of Ann Kampersal.

Tallahassee Community College screen shot reprinted with permission of the Tallahassee Community College Information Technology Department.

TILT screen shot reprinted with permission from the Digital Information Literacy Office on behalf of the University of Texas System Digital Library.

Working with Teens and Loving It screen shot reprinted with permission of the Young Adult Library Services Association, a division of the American Library Association.

Yourhomework.com screen shot reprinted with permission of YourHomework LLC. YourHomework.com provides free services for students, librarians and teachers. Yourhomework. com name and Logo are trademarks of YOURHOMEWORK LLC. All screen shots, content, and graphic image reproduc-

Index

About the Authors

CAROLYN B. NOAH is the administrator of the Central Massachusetts Regional Library System in Shrewsbury, Massachusetts, where she manages a Web-based distance learning program. She currently serves on the board of directors of the Association for Library Services to Children and previously served as the chair of the Intellectual Freedom Committee of the Association and as the president of the New England Library Association.

LINDA W. BRAUN is an educational technology consultant with LEO: Librarians & Educators Online. She works with schools and libraries to provide consulting, training, and project management on a variety of topics. Along with her work for LEO, Linda currently teaches in the Lesley University, Graduate School of Education, Technology in Education program and for the University of Maine in their Library and Information Technology distance education program. She is the author of *Introducing the Internet to Young Learners*: *Ready-To-Go Activities and Lesson Plans* (Neal-Schuman, 2001).